core belief™

Bible Study Series
for junior high/middle school

THE TRUTH ABOUT Suffering

Group
Loveland, Colorado

The Truth About Suffering

Core Belief Bible Study Series

Credits

Editors: Lisa Baba Lauffer and Karl Leuthauser
Managing Editor: Michael D. Warden
Chief Creative Officer: Joani Schultz
Copy Editor: Julie Meiklejohn
Art Director: Lisa Chandler
Cover Art Director: Helen H. Lannis
Cover Designer/Assistant Art Director: Bill Fisher
Computer Graphic Artist: Randy Kady
Photographer: Craig DeMartino
Production Manager: Gingar Kunkel

ISBN 0-7644-0855-0

10 9 8 7 6 5 4 3 2 1 06 05 04 03 02 01 00 99 98 97

Printed in the United States of America.

core belief™

Bible Study Series

for junior high/middle school

contents:

the Core Belief: Suffering

We live in a society that shuns pain. We avoid anything that causes us discomfort, and when we suffer, we wonder what we've done wrong.

Sometimes the answer is "nothing."

Try as we might, we can't stave off the entrance of suffering into our lives. It's a part of our world. From the instant that Eve took that first bite of forbidden fruit, humanity was doomed to suffer. This wasn't part of God's original plan—he had created a perfect world with no sorrow or loss. But with sin came pain and death.

We don't understand it. We try to reconcile the idea of a loving God with the disaster we see in our world and experience in our own lives. But when we stop resisting it and start responding to it with faith in God, he can use suffering to teach us some of the most valuable lessons we'll ever learn.

the Helpful Stuff

the Studies

Suffering as a Core Christian Belief

- Why does God let people starve to death?
- Why do bad things happen to good people?
- How could a loving God let innocent children suffer and die?

It's easy for teenagers to see the suffering around them and question how God could let such things happen.

We don't have all the answers to the problem of suffering, but kids need to be able to work through the questions and discover the answers that the Bible does give. Only then will they be able to affirm their faith in our loving and all-powerful God.

Use the studies in this Core Christian Belief to help your kids grapple with the problem of suffering. When they discover and grasp the answers for themselves, you'll see their faith solidify and grow.

The first study in this book will challenge kids to realize that they aren't alone when they face **life struggles.** Suffering is a normal part of life that everyone goes through. Kids will be encouraged to reach out to God and to others as they work through personal difficulties. They can find that God doesn't initiate their suffering, but he does allow it to happen.

In the second study, kids will be encouraged to see that God is with them when they hurt, even when they are forced to deal with the overwhelming pain that comes with **divorce.** By looking at God's faithfulness during a parental breakup, kids can discover that God is there for them through every kind of trial they may face.

The third study will encourage kids to help others who are suffering from material, emotional, or spiritual **poverty.** Kids can find that they can bring hope to the hurting. God is ready to give them the courage and ability to take action on behalf of others who suffer.

In the fourth study, kids will face one of the most incomprehensible aspects of suffering—a perfect God often brings good out of the hurt and hopelessness of **disappointment.** Although God doesn't cause suffering, he often uses it to turn our hearts from worthless pursuits to a deeper desire to know him. He can use disappointment and all types of suffering to strengthen our character and increase our faith.

Whether we like it or not, suffering is a reality of life. If your kids don't experience it much themselves, they certainly see it around them. And it's an issue that could cause them to reject God if it makes them see him as less than loving. So help your kids deal with this important issue as they learn what the Bible says about God and suffering.

For a more comprehensive look at this Core Christian Belief, read Group's ***Get Real: Making Core Christian Beliefs Relevant to Teenagers.***

DEPTHFINDER

HOW THE BIBLE DESCRIBES SUFFERING

To help you effectively guide your kids toward understanding of this Core Christian Belief, use these overviews as a launching point for a more in-depth study of suffering.

- **Suffering is an intrusion into God's creation.** God created a world free from any pain or suffering. When Adam and Eve sinned, sickness, pain, suffering, and death corrupted creation. Through Jesus' suffering and death on the cross, sin, suffering, and death will ultimately be defeated. When Jesus returns and establishes the new heaven and new earth, Christians will live with him, free from pain and sorrow. (Genesis 1:31; 3:15-19; Job 2:6-7; Isaiah 65:17-20; Romans 8:19-22; and Revelation 21:1-8).
- **Suffering is a mystery for humans.** It's difficult for us to understand how God can be loving and all-powerful but allow faithful followers or innocent children to suffer. So we have three choices: reject the idea that God is loving; reject the idea that God is all-powerful; or accept on faith that our loving, all-powerful God allows suffering for good reasons. (Job 1–3; Psalms 37:7-24; 73:1-20; Romans 8:18-19; and 2 Corinthians 4:16-18; 12:7-10).
- **We suffer because we live in a sin-cursed world.** In general, suffering is a consequence of the sin in our world. For example, the suffering of a group of people—such as a community or a nation—can be the result of the people's sin. Sometimes individuals suffer because of their leaders' or their parents' sins. And sometimes an individual's suffering results from the individual's sin. God may also allow suffering in order to discipline people, much as a human parent might discipline a child to correct wrong behavior (Numbers 14:31-33; Psalm 119:67; Jeremiah 13:21-27; Luke 13:1-5; Acts 5:1-11; 1 Corinthians 11:29-30; and Galatians 6:7-8).

- **Suffering is a part of human redemption.** Jesus had to suffer to make eternal life and peace with God possible for us. To defeat sin and suffering for our sake, Jesus had to endure tremendous suffering and rejection, even though he had never sinned. He suffered in our place so that we might one day be free from all suffering (Luke 9:22; 24:46; Acts 17:3; 26:22-23; Hebrews 2:10-15; 9:24-28; and 1 Peter 3:18).
- **Suffering can be a means of spiritual growth.** Like Jesus, Christians are called to suffer in this life. But God promises to be with us through it all. To God, our faith and obedience are more important than our comfort. And sometimes suffering is necessary to produce a more faithful, enduring follower (Psalm 66:8-12; Matthew 28:20; Romans 5:3-5; 8:28, 34-39; 2 Corinthians 12:7-10; James 1:2-4, 12; and 1 Peter 1:6-9).
- **Suffering can allow us to participate in Jesus' suffering.** Faithful Christians who suffer for their faith should view that suffering as a privilege. We share in Jesus' suffering when we are persecuted because of our faith in him. Our suffering doesn't make us more righteous, but through it we can demonstrate and strengthen our faith in Jesus by enduring our suffering with joy. We can be confident that God doesn't allow the burden of suffering without also providing the strength to stand up under it (Matthew 16:24-25; Acts 5:41-42; 20:22-24; Romans 8:17; Philippians 1:27-30; 3:10; and 1 Peter 4:1-2, 13-14).
- **God wants us to respond to suffering with faith.** Christians, like everyone else, will experience suffering in this life. But as followers of God, we're to respond to suffering by striving to draw closer to God. For example, when we suffer we should ask God for wisdom or insight into the cause. We should confess any known sin and cry out to God for strength or relief (Psalms 10; 13; 35; 51:1-12; 142; and James 1:5).

CORE CHRISTIAN BELIEF OVERVIEW

Here are the twenty-four Core Christian Belief categories that form the backbone of Core Belief Bible Study Series:

The Nature of God	Jesus Christ	The Holy Spirit
Humanity	Evil	Suffering
Creation	The Spiritual Realm	The Bible
Salvation	Spiritual Growth	Personal Character
God's Justice	Sin & Forgiveness	The Last Days
Love	The Church	Worship
Authority	Prayer	Family
Service	Relationships	Sharing Faith

Look for Group's Core Belief Bible Study Series books in these other Core Christian Beliefs!

about core belief

Bible Study Series

for junior high/middle school

Think for a moment about your young people. When your students walk out of your youth program after they graduate from junior high or high school, what do you want them to know? What foundation do you want them to have so they can make wise choices?

You probably want them to know the essentials of the Christian faith. You want them to base everything they do on the foundational truths of Christianity. Are you meeting this goal?

If you have any doubt that your kids will walk into adulthood knowing and living by the tenets of the Christian faith, then you've picked up the right book. All the books in Group's Core Belief Bible Study Series encourage young people to discover the essentials of Christianity and to put those essentials into practice. Let us explain . . .

What Is Group's Core Belief Bible Study Series?

Group's Core Belief Bible Study Series is a biblically in-depth study series for junior high and senior high teenagers. This Bible study series utilizes four defining commitments to create each study. These "plumb lines" provide structure and continuity for every activity, study, project, and discussion. They are:

- **A Commitment to Biblical Depth**—Core Belief Bible Study Series is founded on the belief that kids not only *can* understand the deeper truths of the Bible but also *want* to understand them. Therefore, the activities and studies in this series strive to explain the "why" behind every truth we explore. That way, kids learn principles, not just rules.
- **A Commitment to Relevance**—Most kids aren't interested in abstract theories or doctrines about the universe. They want to know how to live successfully right now, today, in the heat of problems they can't ignore. Because of this, each study connects a real-life need with biblical principles that speak directly to that need. This study series finally bridges the gap between Bible truths and the real-world issues kids face.
- **A Commitment to Variety**—Today's young people have been raised in a sound bite world. They demand variety. For that reason, no two meetings in this study series are shaped exactly the same.
- **A Commitment to Active and Interactive Learning**—Active learning is learning by doing. Interactive learning simply takes active learning a step further by having kids teach each other what they've learned. It's a process that helps kids internalize and remember their discoveries.

For a more detailed description of these concepts, see the section titled "Why Active and Interactive Learning Works With Teenagers" beginning on page 57.

So how can you accomplish all this in a set of four easy-to-lead Bible studies? By weaving together various "power" elements to produce a fun experience that leaves kids challenged and encouraged.

Turn the page to take a look at some of the power elements used in this series.

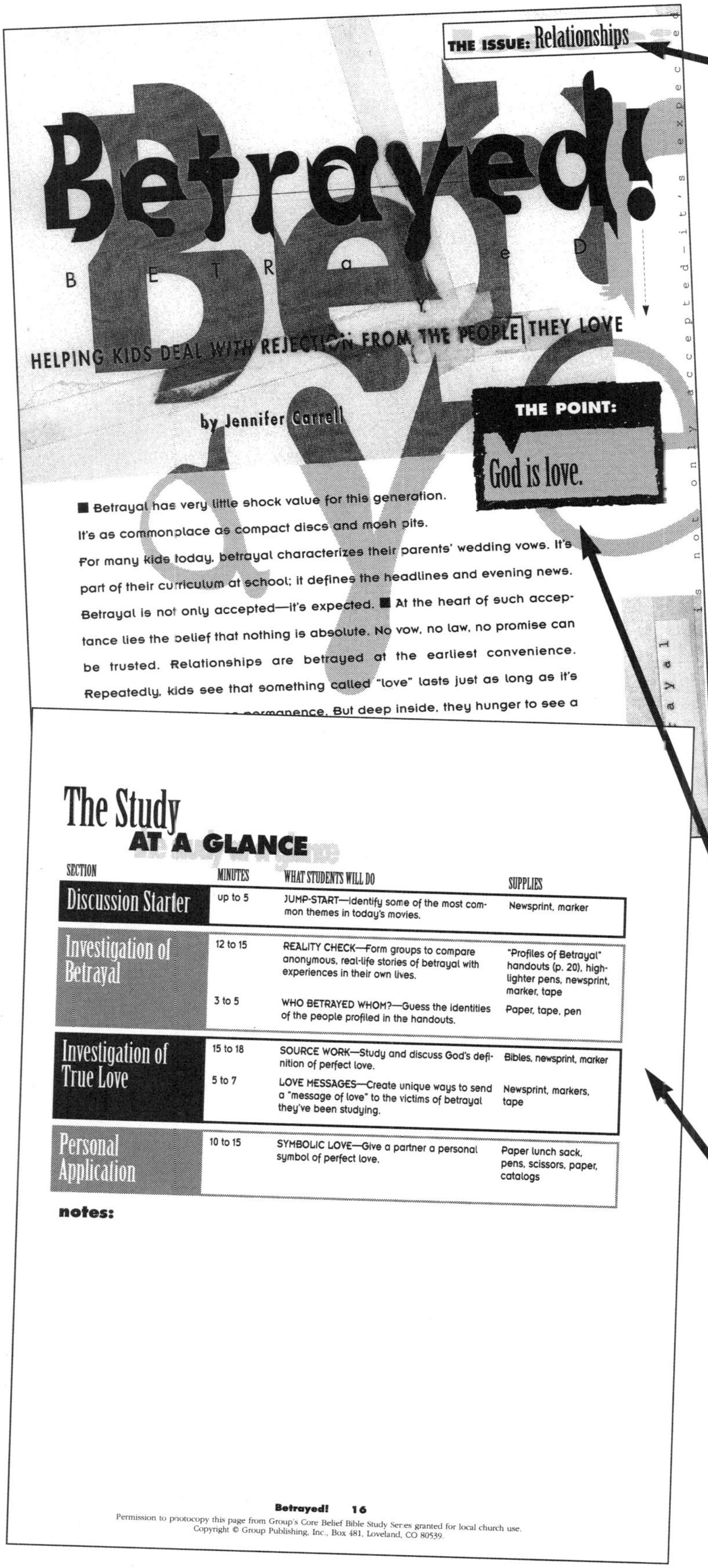

THE ISSUE: Relationships

Betrayed!

HELPING KIDS DEAL WITH REJECTION FROM THE PEOPLE THEY LOVE

by Jennifer Carrell

THE POINT:

God is love.

■ Betrayal has very little shock value for this generation. It's as commonplace as compact discs and mosh pits. For many kids today, betrayal characterizes their parents' wedding vows. It's part of their curriculum at school; it defines the headlines and evening news. Betrayal is not only accepted—it's expected. ■ At the heart of such acceptance lies the belief that nothing is absolute. No vow, no law, no promise can be trusted. Relationships are betrayed at the earliest convenience. Repeatedly, kids see that something called "love" lasts just as long as it's ... permanence. But deep inside, they hunger to see a

The Study AT A GLANCE

SECTION	MINUTES	WHAT STUDENTS WILL DO	SUPPLIES
Discussion Starter	up to 5	JUMP-START—Identify some of the most common themes in today's movies.	Newsprint, marker
Investigation of Betrayal	12 to 15	REALITY CHECK—Form groups to compare anonymous, real-life stories of betrayal with experiences in their own lives.	"Profiles of Betrayal" handouts (p. 20), highlighter pens, newsprint, marker, tape
	3 to 5	WHO BETRAYED WHOM?—Guess the identities of the people profiled in the handouts.	Paper, tape, pen
Investigation of True Love	15 to 18	SOURCE WORK—Study and discuss God's definition of perfect love.	Bibles, newsprint, marker
	5 to 7	LOVE MESSAGES—Create unique ways to send a "message of love" to the victims of betrayal they've been studying.	Newsprint, markers, tape
Personal Application	10 to 15	SYMBOLIC LOVE—Give a partner a personal symbol of perfect love.	Paper lunch sack, pens, scissors, paper, catalogs

notes:

Betrayed! 16

Permission to photocopy this page from Group's Core Belief Bible Study Series granted for local church use. Copyright © Group Publishing, Inc., Box 481, Loveland, CO 80539.

- **A Relevant Topic—**More than ever before, kids live in the now. What matters to them and what attracts their hearts is what's happening in their world at this moment. For this reason, every Core Belief Bible Study focuses on a particular hot topic that kids care about.

- **A Core Christian Belief—**Group's Core Belief Bible Study Series organizes the wealth of Christian truth and experience into twenty-four Core Christian Belief categories. These twenty-four headings act as umbrellas for a collection of detailed beliefs that define Christianity and set it apart from the world and every other religion. Each book in this series features one Core Christian Belief with lessons suited for junior high or senior high students.

  "But," you ask, "won't my kids be bored talking about all these spiritual beliefs?" No way! As a youth leader, you know the value of using hot topics to connect with young people. Ultimately teenagers talk about issues because they're searching for meaning in their lives. They want to find the one equation that will make sense of all the confusing events happening around them. Each Core Belief Bible Study answers that need by connecting a hot topic with a powerful Christian principle. Kids walk away from the study with something more solid than just the shifting ebb and flow of their own opinions. They walk away with a deeper understanding of their Christian faith.

- **The Point—**This simple statement is designed to be the intersection between the Core Christian Belief and the hot topic. Everything in the study ultimately focuses on The Point so that kids study it and allow it time to sink into their hearts.

- **The Study at a Glance—**A quick look at this chart will tell you what kids will do, how long it will take them to do it, and what supplies you'll need to get it done.

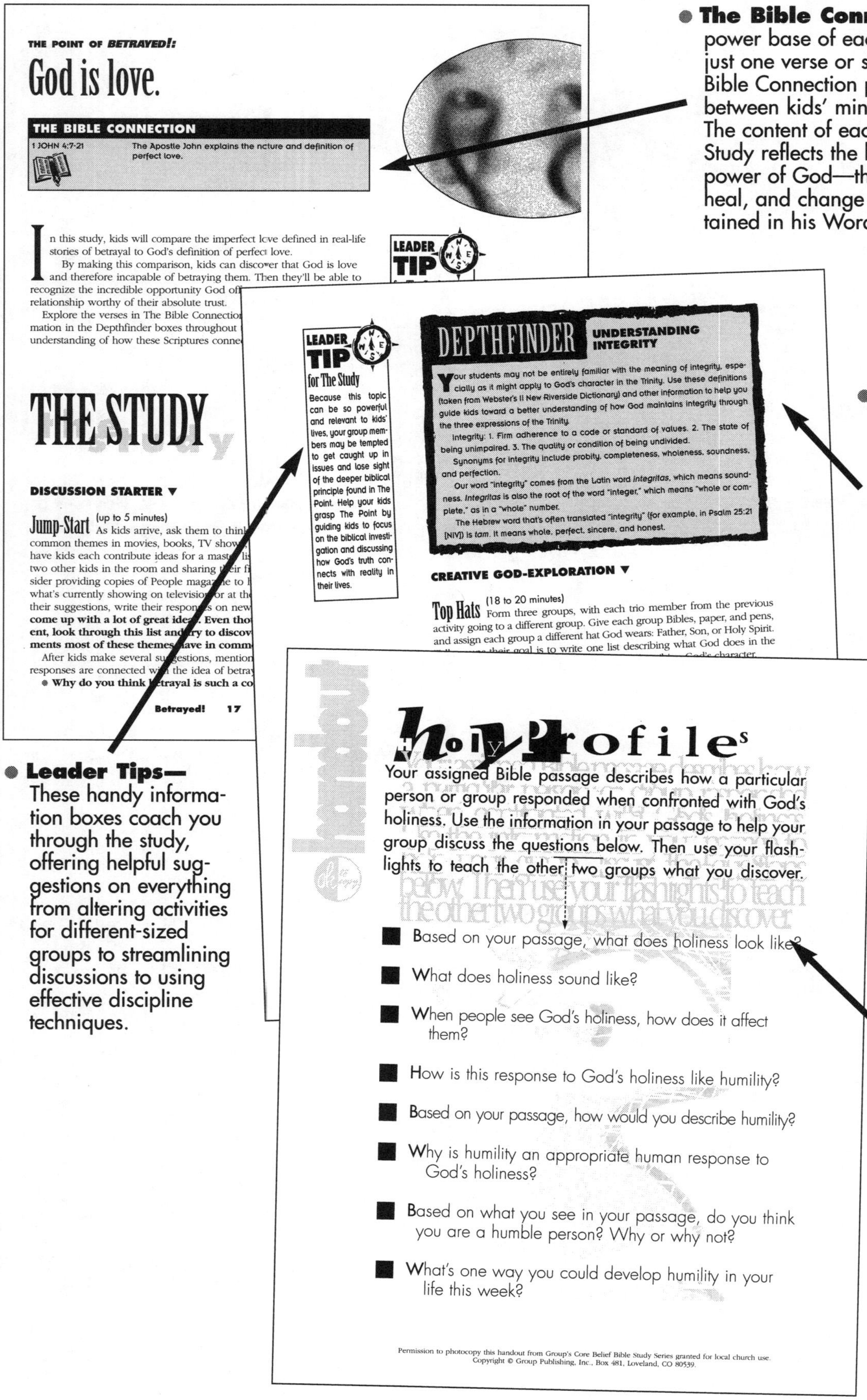
THE POINT OF *BETRAYED!*:

God is love.

THE BIBLE CONNECTION

1 JOHN 4:7-21 — The Apostle John explains the ncture and definition of perfect love.

In this study, kids will compare the imperfect love defined in real-life stories of betrayal to God's definition of perfect love.

By making this comparison, kids can discover that God is love and therefore incapable of betraying them. Then they'll be able to recognize the incredible opportunity God off... relationship worthy of their absolute trust.

Explore the verses in The Bible Connectio... mation in the Depthfinder boxes throughout ... understanding of how these Scriptures conne...

THE STUDY

DISCUSSION STARTER ▼

Jump-Start (up to 5 minutes) As kids arrive, ask them to think... common themes in movies, books, TV show... have kids each contribute ideas for a mast... two other kids in the room and sharing their... sider providing copies of People magazine to h... what's currently showing on television or at th... their suggestions, write their responses on new... **come up with a lot of great ideas. Even tho... ent, look through this list and try to discov... ments most of these themes have in comm...**

After kids make several suggestions, mention... responses are connected with the idea of betray...

● **Why do you think betrayal is such a co...**

Betrayed! 17

LEADER TIP for The Study

Because this topic can be so powerful and relevant to kids' lives, your group members may be tempted to get caught up in issues and lose sight of the deeper biblical principle found in The Point. Help your kids grasp The Point by guiding kids to focus on the biblical investigation and discussing how God's truth connects with reality in their lives.

DEPTHFINDER — UNDERSTANDING INTEGRITY

Your students may not be entirely familiar with the meaning of integrity, especially as it might apply to God's character in the Trinity. Use these definitions (taken from Webster's II New Riverside Dictionary) and other information to help you guide kids toward a better understanding of how God maintains integrity through the three expressions of the Trinity.

Integrity: 1. Firm adherence to a code or standard of values. 2. The state of being unimpaired. 3. The quality or condition of being undivided.

Synonyms for integrity include probity, completeness, wholeness, soundness, and perfection.

Our word "integrity" comes from the Latin word *integritas*, which means soundness. *Integritas* is also the root of the word "integer," which means "whole or complete," as in a "whole" number.

The Hebrew word that's often translated "integrity" (for example, in Psalm 25:21 [NIV]) is *tam*. It means whole, perfect, sincere, and honest.

CREATIVE GOD-EXPLORATION ▼

Top Hats (18 to 20 minutes) Form three groups, with each trio member from the previous activity going to a different group. Give each group Bibles, paper, and pens, and assign each group a different hat God wears: Father, Son, or Holy Spirit. ...

handout

Holy Profiles

Your assigned Bible passage describes how a particular person or group responded when confronted with God's holiness. Use the information in your passage to help your group discuss the questions below. Then use your flashlights to teach the other two groups what you discover.

- Based on your passage, what does holiness look like?
- What does holiness sound like?
- When people see God's holiness, how does it affect them?
- How is this response to God's holiness like humility?
- Based on your passage, how would you describe humility?
- Why is humility an appropriate human response to God's holiness?
- Based on what you see in your passage, do you think you are a humble person? Why or why not?
- What's one way you could develop humility in your life this week?

Permission to photocopy this handout from Group's Core Belief Bible Study Series granted for local church use. Copyright © Group Publishing, Inc., Box 481, Loveland, CO 80539.

● **The Bible Connection—**This is the power base of each study. Whether it's just one verse or several chapters, The Bible Connection provides the vital link between kids' minds and their hearts. The content of each Core Belief Bible Study reflects the belief that the true power of God—the power to expose, heal, and change kids' lives—is contained in his Word.

● **Depthfinder Boxes—**These informative sidelights located throughout each study add insight into a particular passage, word, historical fact, or Christian doctrine. Depthfinder boxes also provide insight into teen culture, adolescent development, current events, and philosophy.

● **Leader Tips—**These handy information boxes coach you through the study, offering helpful suggestions on everything from altering activities for different-sized groups to streamlining discussions to using effective discipline techniques.

● **Handouts—**Most Core Belief Bible Studies include photocopiable handouts to use with your group. Handouts might take the form of a fun game, a lively discussion starter, or a challenging study page for kids to take home—anything to make your study more meaningful and effective.

The Last Word on Core Belief Bible Studies

Soon after you begin to use Group's Core Belief Bible Study Series, you'll see signs of real growth in your group members. Your kids will gain a deeper understanding of the Bible and of their own Christian faith. They'll see more clearly how a relationship with Jesus affects their daily lives. And they'll grow closer to God.

But that's not all. You'll also see kids grow closer to one another.

That's because this series is founded on the principle that Christian faith grows best in the context of relationship. Each study uses a variety of interactive pairs and small groups and always includes discussion questions that promote deeper relationships. The friendships kids will build through this study series will enable them to grow *together* toward a deeper relationship with God.

Why Do Bad Things Happen to Me?

by Lisa Baba Lauffer

THE POINT:

Suffering is a normal part of life.

■ "Hello, and welcome to the Wheel of Misfortune, the game show where you spin the wheel and discover what disasters will befall you. Today's contestants will spin the wheel to see if they'll encounter trials such as volcanic eruptions, hurricanes, divorced parents, floods, broken limbs, typhoons, cancer, and the Big One—the 10.0 earthquake! You needn't enter to win—you're already playing just by being alive. So before you take another step, spin the wheel!" ■ Some game—one you'd choose to avoid at all costs, right? But here's the bad news—you don't have a choice, and it's not a game. Every day people experience heartbreak—it's an unavoidable part of the world we live in. The only variable is when suffering will make its bold, devastating entrance into your life and your students' lives. ■ This study explores the reality that we all suffer and encourages students to help each other through their hard times.

The Study AT A GLANCE

SECTION	MINUTES	WHAT STUDENTS WILL DO	SUPPLIES
Opener	5 to 10	SQUIRTIN' HURTIN'—Pass a mound of shaving cream to each other.	Shaving cream
Graph Creation	15 to 20	GRAPHIC PAIN—Create a graph on the wall representing the level of each individual's pain and the connection the group has in pain.	"Suffering Gauge" handouts (p. 23), pencils, index cards, tape, yarn, chair or stepladder
Bible Discovery	10 to 15	PAIN PORTRAITS—Study the story of Mephibosheth and rank his pain on the graph.	"Mephibosheth's Ups and Downs" Depthfinder (p. 20), pencils, yarn, tape
	5 to 10	PAIN GAINS—Create symbols representing positive outcomes of suffering.	Bibles, objects in the meeting room, tape
Application	5 to 10	LEAN ON ME CLUB—Create an opportunity to help each other through struggles.	Suffering Gauges from the "Graphic Pain" activity, pencils, box or basket

notes:

• need
✓ - shaving cream
- photostate "suffering gauge"
- wool + tape
✓ - write questions + photostate
✓ - paper 4 pain rating

THE POINT OF *WHY DO BAD THINGS HAPPEN TO ME?*:

Suffering is a normal part of life.

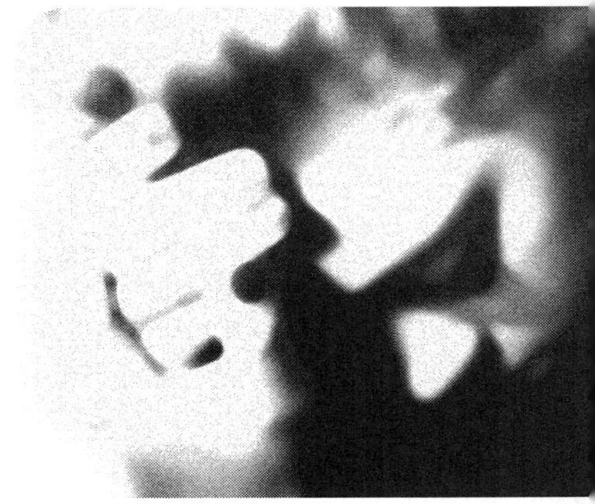

THE BIBLE CONNECTION

2 SAMUEL 4:4; 9:1-13; 16:1-4; 19:24-30; 21:7	These passages relate the story of Mephibosheth's joy and suffering.
ROMANS 5:3-5; JAMES 1:2-4	These passages express how we can grow spiritually and emotionally through our trials.

In this study, kids will create a larger-than-life graph representing the level of pain they experience. Then they'll compare their pain level to the pain experienced by Mephibosheth (me-FIB-o-sheth), King Saul's grandson. Kids will also explore Scripture passages describing positive results of painful times.

By creating the graph and exploring Scripture passages, kids can learn why pain is a normal part of their lives.

Explore the verses in The Bible Connection, then examine the information in the Depthfinder boxes throughout the study to gain a deeper understanding of how these Scriptures connect with your young people.

LEADER TIP for The Study

Whenever you tell groups to discuss a list of questions, write the questions on newsprint and tape the newsprint to the wall so groups can answer the questions at their own pace.

THE STUDY

OPENER ▼

Squirtin' Hurtin' (5 to 10 minutes)

Have kids form two teams, and have each team stand in a circle. Squirt a softball-sized mound of shaving cream into the hands of one student on each team. Say: **We're going to have a race based not on time but on the amount of "clean." Your task is to pass the shaving cream around your circle, leaving as little of it on your hands as possible. This is a team event—at the end of**

LEADER TIP for Squirtin' Hurtin'

Have rags and a large bowl of water available so kids can clean up after the race.

LEADER TIP for The Study

Because this topic can be so powerful and relevant to kids' lives, your group members may be tempted to get caught up in issues and lose sight of the deeper biblical principle found in The Point. Help your kids grasp The Point by guiding kids to focus on the biblical investigation and discussing how God's truth connects with reality in their lives.

the race I'll determine a winner by looking at the shaving cream left on all team members' hands. Remember, you can only use your hands to pass the shaving cream. Ready? Go!

After the race, have kids hold up their hands palms out. Judge which team has the least shaving cream on everyone's hands, and declare the winning team. Then have kids form pairs to discuss these questions:

- **How is trying to avoid getting shaving cream on your hands like trying to avoid suffering?**
- **Have you ever tried to avoid suffering? If so, how?**
- **What are other ways you've dealt with suffering?**

Say: **The shaving cream in this activity is like suffering in real life—try as you might, you just can't avoid it. Today we're going to explore how suffering is a normal part of life.**

Allow kids to wash their hands before the next activity.

DEPTHFINDER — UNDERSTANDING THE BIBLE

Romans 5:3-5 and James 1:2-4 describe benefits that come from enduring trials—patience, character, hope, and perfected faith. Here are a few Bible characters who illustrate positive results of suffering:

- Joseph—his brothers sold him into slavery, but he eventually saved his whole family from famine (Genesis 37–45).
- Ruth—her husband died, but she married again and became an ancestor of Jesus Christ (Ruth 1–4; Matthew 1:5-16).
- Paul—he was imprisoned for sharing his faith, and others became bold in sharing the Gospel (Philippians 1:12-14).

If you have a student enduring a difficult trial, copy this Depthfinder and encourage your student to use it for Bible study. Through reading the stories of these Bible characters, your student may gain strength to endure his or her own hardships.

LEADER TIP for Graphic Pain

When kids talk with the people on both sides, the kids on the ends will only have one person beside them. Have these two kids share with each other as well as the people next to them.

GRAPH CREATION ▼

Graphic Pain

(15 to 20 minutes)

Say: **Let's create a graph that illustrates the level of pain in our lives.**

Give each student a copy of the "Suffering Gauge" handout (p. 23), a pencil, and an index card. Say: **Follow the directions on the Suffering Gauge to determine your Total Pain Ranking. Rate from one to ten (ten being the highest) the level of suffering you experience in the three areas listed. For example, if you feel a lot of pain at home because your parents just divorced, you might rank pain from your family at nine. If your family life is pretty happy right now, you might rank pain from your family at two. When you've rated all three areas, add the scores and divide the sum by**

three. You'll then have your Total Pain Ranking.

Give your students a minute to fill out their Suffering Gauges. Then say: **Write your name and Total Pain Ranking on your index card.**

Have kids stand in a line along the walls of your meeting room. Make sure they stand a foot apart and face you. Hand each student a piece of tape, and say: **We're going to create a graph on the walls of our room to illustrate the amount of pain we're all feeling. Let's say that the floor of the room represents the number one and the ceiling represents the number ten. Tape your index card to the wall at the level representing your Total Pain Ranking. For example, if your Total Pain Ranking is seven, tape the card to the wall about two-thirds of the way from the floor.**

When kids have finished, have them share with the people on both sides one way they're suffering. For example, kids might say that they just put a favorite pet to sleep, their parents argue a lot, or they're struggling with their grades.

As kids talk, cut a ten foot length of yarn for each student. Give each student a piece of yarn and two pieces of tape. Say: **Connect your card with the card of the person on your right. Tape one end of your yarn to your card and the other end to theirs. As you do this, tell that person a gift you wish you could give them to help them through their pain. For example, if the person next to you suffers because the bully at school picks on him or her, you could say, "I wish I could give you a shield to protect you from that bully."** Have a stepladder or chair available to help kids tape their cards to the wall.

When the graph is complete, have kids form trios to discuss these questions:

- **What do you think the average level of pain is in this room?**
- **Based on this graph, is your Total Pain Ranking below average, average, or above average? What's your reaction to that?**
- **Are you surprised by any of the cards up there? If so, which one(s) and why?**
- **What does our graph tell you about pain and suffering?**

Say: **As you can see from our graph, we all experience suffering. Even if today you're at "one," there will be another day when you're at "five" or maybe even "ten." We all suffer because suffering is a normal part of life.**

POINT

BIBLE DISCOVERY ▼

Pain Portraits (10 to 15 minutes)

Give each trio a pencil and a copy of the "Mephibosheth's Ups and Downs" Depthfinder (p. 20). Have kids read the handouts and the passages listed on them. Then have trios discuss this question:

- **What do you think Mephibosheth's Total Pain Ranking would be on a scale of one to ten?**

Have trios tell their Total Pain Rankings for Mephibosheth and explain why they chose that number. Take the average of their Total

LEADER TIP for Graphic Pain

Suffering is a difficult topic to discuss, especially when kids (and adults!) examine their own pain. If your kids seem agitated during this activity, have them sit down and discuss these questions:

- **What is it about the topic of suffering that makes you not want to concentrate on creating this graph?**
- **What makes talking about suffering so hard?**
- **What would help you feel more comfortable with discussing this topic today?**

If feasible, allow your kids to do what they answered in the last question. Then proceed with the meeting.

DEPTHFINDER

MEPHIBOSHETH'S UPS AND DOWNS

We all have our ups and downs, and Mephibosheth had them, too. Read the following list and the Bible passages next to each entry to discover Mephibosheth's joy and suffering:

- Mephibosheth's father and grandfather were killed in battle (2 Samuel 1:4; 4:4).
- Mephibosheth was crippled at the age of five (2 Samuel 4:4).
- King David honored Mephibosheth by declaring that he would always eat at the king's table and that Ziba, the king's servant, would care for him (2 Samuel 9:1-13).
- Ziba betrayed Mephibosheth by lying to King David and saying that Mephibosheth had betrayed the king (2 Samuel 16:1-4).
- King David gave Mephibosheth a chance to explain his side (2 Samuel 19:24-28).
- King David told Mephibosheth to split his land with Ziba, the person who had betrayed him (2 Samuel 19:29).
- Mephibosheth declared his loyalty to the king (2 Samuel 19:30).
- King David spared Mephibosheth when his enemies wanted to kill him and his relatives (2 Samuel 21:7).

Pain Rankings, and have the entire group help tape yarn to the wall at the level of that number, extending the yarn across the entire graph. Then have kids return to their trios to discuss these questions:

- **How does Mephibosheth's Total Pain Ranking compare to yours? What's your reaction to that?**
- **On a scale of one to ten, how fair was all the suffering Mephibosheth experienced?**
- **How did Mephibosheth's relationship with David affect Mephibosheth's level of suffering?**
- **Of the bad things that happen to you, how many of them are fair? Why?**
- **Do you have anyone to help you endure your suffering? If so, who is it, and how does that person help you? If not, how could you develop a relationship with someone who could help you?**

Say: **As the story of Mephibosheth shows, suffering is a normal part of life. Mephibosheth didn't deserve to lose his father and grandfather or to be crippled—these things just happened to him. He had to learn to deal with his misfortunes. But as he lived through his trials, he developed a relationship with David. David helped him to endure the things that brought him pain.**

Have trios pray, with each person asking God to help their partners with their struggles.

Pain Gains

(5 to 10 minutes)

Say: **We don't like to feel pain, and it's hard to accept that it's a normal part of life. But what if we can gain some good from it? What might be positive results of our pain?**

Have trios read Romans 5:3-5 and James 1:2-4 and discuss these questions:

- **According to these Bible verses, what are some positive results of pain?**
- **What are specific positive results you've experienced from your own suffering? For example, maybe you're learning to be more independent because your parents divorced.**

Have trios create at least one symbol that represents a positive result of a painful situation. Kids can use anything in the room such as chairs, index cards, and Bibles to create their symbols. For example, kids might open a Bible to express that they grew closer to God through suffering.

Have trios show their symbols to the whole group and explain what they represent. Then have trios either set their symbols on the floor beneath the graph or tape their symbols to the wall somewhere under the yarn line.

Say: **Even though we don't like to suffer, we can all gain something good from our pain. God is with us when we suffer, and he can help us learn from our trials. Just as suffering is a normal part of life, growing through pain can be normal, too.**

APPLICATION ▼

Lean on Me Club

(5 to 10 minutes)

Say: **Even though pain can bring good things into our lives, it still hurts. We need people to be with us through our suffering, just as David helped Mephibosheth through his painful times. Although suffering is a normal part of life, we can make suffering more bearable by being there for each other.**

Have kids write on the back of their Suffering Gauge handouts one way a friend could help them through their suffering.

Then say: **Because suffering is a normal part of life, we need to learn to deal with it. As we learned from Mephibosheth's story, it always helps to have people help you through your suffering. So we're going to create a Lean on Me Club. Everyone can choose to join, but you don't have to. If you want to join, check the Lean on Me box that's at the bottom left corner of your Suffering Gauge handout. We'll put all the handouts in a box** (or basket). **If you checked the Lean on Me box on your Suffering Gauge (and only if you checked the box), I'll pair you with someone who has a struggle similar to yours. Next week, I'll tell you who your partner is and give you that person's Suffering Gauge. Then you can help your partners through their pain by doing what's written on the back of their Suffering Gauges.** After kids have had a chance to check the Lean on Me boxes, have them put their Suffering Gauges in a box or basket.

After the meeting, use the Suffering Gauges to pair students coping with similar issues. For example, one person may feel rejected by a friend, and another just broke up with a girlfriend—both students feel the loss of a valued relationship. At your next meeting, tell students who their partners are and remind them to do what's written on the back of their partners' Suffering Gauges.

LEADER TIP for Lean on Me Club

If kids want to choose their own partners, have students meet with you after the study to make their choices.

DEPTHFINDER

UNDERSTANDING THESE KIDS

The Garden of Eden—that's where suffering began. Adam and Eve couldn't resist the temptation to eat forbidden fruit, and the world has been suffering ever since. Violence, sickness, poverty, death—all are results of that brief, prideful moment of disobedience.

Perhaps more than any other generation, today's generation of kids feel the brunt of the sinful nature of our world. More life and death issues face this generation than have faced any generation before it. According to Rob Nelson and Jon Cowan, authors of *Revolution X: A Survival Guide for Our Generation*, here are some worldly realities that make suffering a normal part of life for today's young people.

- Today's young person is twice as likely to die by suicide or homicide as a teenager in 1960.
- Since 1961, violent crime in America has increased by 560 percent.
- Since 1961, births to unwed mothers have increased by 400 percent.
- Every year, factories contaminate our air, land, and water by belching three million tons of toxic chemicals into our atmosphere.
- About sixty people a day are killed with handguns.
- Over 2,500 American kids a day see their parents separate or divorce.
- Ninety kids a day are put into foster homes.
- The rate of youth arrests for violent crimes has risen 91 percent since 1970.
- Over 20 percent of American kids live in poverty.

handout

Name: ______________________

Suffering GAUGE

On a scale from one to ten (one being the lowest and ten being the highest), rank the amount of pain you experience in your life because of:

YOUR FAMILY	
YOUR FRIENDS	
SCHOOL	
ADD YOUR THREE RANKINGS HERE	
DIVIDE YOUR TOTAL BY THREE	÷ 3
THIS NUMBER IS YOUR TOTAL PAIN RANKING	

In comparison to the rest of the class, do you think your Total Pain Ranking is (circle one):

BELOW AVERAGE? AVERAGE? ABOVE AVERAGE?

☐ LEAN ON ME

but God never leaves

The Lives of Kids From Families Ripped Apart

by Stephen Parolini

Intro ①

■ Average family. ■ What's the first image that comes to mind when you hear that phrase? Not too long ago, you may have pictured the suburban home with Mom, Dad, the 2.6 children, and the dog. You know—the Cleavers from *Leave It to Beaver* or the Taylors from *Home Improvement*. ■ But nowadays, the term "average family" merely confuses. After all, what's the typical family structure these days? Mom, Dad, and 2.6 kids? Or the single father struggling to connect with his son and daughter? The single mother striving to financially support her children? The newly remarried couple attempting to blend two sets of children into one family? ■ Think of your young people. What kinds of families do they come from? ■ This study helps kids discover that even if their families break up, God will never leave them, and he will help them endure their hurts.

THE POINT:

God is with you when you hurt.

today – God never leaves!

The Study AT A GLANCE

SECTION	MINUTES	WHAT STUDENTS WILL DO	SUPPLIES
Creative Opener	10 to 15	THE SOUND OF DIVORCE—Create sounds to express how abandonment feels.	Objects in the meeting room
Bible Exploration	15 to 20	I'M OUTTA HERE—Build "stable homes" from index cards.	Bibles, index cards, paper, pencils
Reflection	10 to 15	BEING THERE—Arrange index cards on the floor to indicate times parents and friends have been there for them.	Bibles, index cards, masking tape, pencils, yarn
Commitment Time	10 to 15	I'M HERE—Create support teams for future times of need.	Bibles, "Being There" handout (p. 33), pencils, scissors

notes:

NEED:

- cards
- big paper 4 questions (in 4's)
- little paper →
- masking tape

THE POINT OF *BUT GOD NEVER LEAVES:*

God is with you when you hurt.

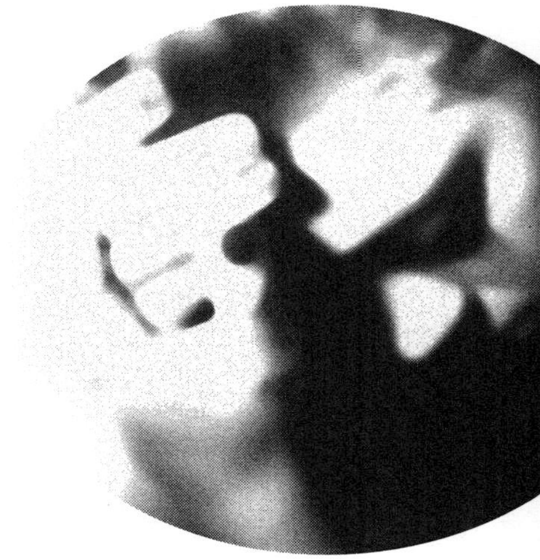

THE BIBLE CONNECTION	
RUTH 1:1-18; JOB 1:13-22; MATTHEW 27:45-50; JOHN 16:32-33	These passages describe times various Bible characters felt abandoned.
PSALM 145:17-20; MATTHEW 28:20	These passages describe God's promises to always be with those who love him.

In this study, kids will creatively express the painful feelings that arise from divorce. Then they'll explore Scriptures describing Bible characters who felt abandoned and God's presence when we feel abandoned.

Through this exploration, kids will discover that God is always with them, especially when they hurt.

Explore the verses in The Bible Connection, then examine the information in the Depthfinder boxes throughout the study to gain a deeper understanding of how these Scriptures connect with your young people.

LEADER TIP for The Study

Whenever you tell groups to discuss a list of questions, write the questions on newsprint and tape the newsprint to the wall so groups can answer the questions at their own pace.

THE STUDY

CREATIVE OPENER ▼

The Sound of Divorce

(10 to 15 minutes)

When all of your kids have arrived, say: **Today we're going to explore the subjects of divorce and abandonment. To start, find two other people and tell each other a time when you felt abandoned. For example, you might have felt**

LEADER TIP for The Sound of Divorce

If you have more than twelve students in your class, have kids form pairs or trios and create their sounds of pain in these small groups.

LEADER TIP for The Study

Because this topic can be so powerful and relevant to kids' lives, your group members may be tempted to get caught up in issues and lose sight of the deeper biblical principle found in The Point. Help your kids grasp The Point by guiding kids to focus on the biblical investigation and discussing how God's truth connects with reality in their lives.

DEPTH FINDER — UNDERSTANDING THE BIBLE

While the story told in Ruth 1:1-18 isn't about divorce, it's still a biblical example of feeling abandoned. Naomi lost her husband and her two sons. She and her two daughters-in-law, Orpah and Ruth, were left widowed and childless. Not only did these women have to deal with grief from their losses, they also had to contend with their culture—a culture that granted women value only in relation to their husbands and children. Left completely alone and without cultural value, all three of these women were totally dependent on the charity of others.

Only a few junior highers today may suffer the feelings of abandonment that come with the death of a parent, relative, or friend. Yet many experience feelings of abandonment due to divorce or separation of their parents. Mother or father leaves home, and even if the divorce is on good terms, kids are left with holes in their hearts. While our culture isn't as tough on kids from divorced homes as Naomi's culture was on widowed, childless women, kids know that their families aren't completely accepted in society.

If you have students who feel abandoned through divorce, death, or other circumstances, encourage them to read the rest of Naomi, Orpah, and Ruth's story found in the book of Ruth. Through this story, kids can discover how God is with them when they hurt and how God can take the bleakest stories and create happy endings for them.

abandoned when a friend moved away, your parents divorced or separated, or a relative died.

When kids have finished, say: **What does divorce feel like to you? To answer that question, invent a sound that expresses the pain of divorce. You may create your sound using objects in this room, such as chairs, pencils, trash cans, paper, and books. You may also use words or other sounds you create with your voice. You'll each have an opportunity to "perform" your sound for the rest of the class.**

After two minutes, invite kids to perform their sounds for the rest of the group. Encourage kids to be silent and respectful when other students perform their sounds. Then have all kids perform their sounds at the same time.

Have trios discuss the following questions:

- **What was it like to express your feelings through sound?**
- **How did these sounds communicate the pain of divorce?**
- **How do these sounds resemble how it feels to come from a "broken home"? how it feels to hear about someone else's parents separating or divorcing?**

Invite volunteers to share their trios' insights with the whole group. Then say: **Your sounds express how horrible the pain of divorce feels. Maybe you come from a broken home. If so, you know how it feels to be separated from someone you love. But even if you don't come from a divorced family, you can still feel the pain of abandonment.**

As we talk about broken homes today, think of how you felt when your parents divorced, when a friend's parents divorced, or when somebody important to you left. This won't be an easy topic to discuss, but it's important. Through today's study, you'll discover

how God is with you when you hurt.

Before we begin our next activity, let's pray. Silently ask God to prepare you for today's study. Then ask God to show you how he's with you when you hurt. Allow kids one minute to pray silently.

BIBLE EXPLORATION ▼

I'm Outta Here (15 to 20 minutes)

Say: **To start our exploration, let's build card towers that represent stable homes.** Have kids form pairs, and give each pair fifty or more index cards. Then explain that partners must work together to build a "stable home" using only the index cards and their imaginations.

One minute after pairs begin building their homes, single out one person in each pair to leave. Do this by whispering to each of these people: **I need you to leave your partner and come with me—don't say why you're leaving.** Have an adult volunteer take these kids to another room or into the hall and ask them these questions:

- **What does it feel like to leave your partner in the middle of this activity?**
- **How is this like what happens when someone leaves a spouse and children because of separation or divorce? How is it different?**

Don't explain to the rest of the kids why their partners left. If they protest, just encourage them to continue building their stable homes. Two minutes after each pair has been split, call everyone back together. Have kids pair up with their original partners, then have each pair find another pair to form a foursome. Have foursomes discuss the following questions:

- **How does your card house represent a stable home? a broken home?**
- **What was it like to be suddenly abandoned during this project?**
- **What was it like to suddenly leave your partner all alone?**
- **How was one of you leaving during this project like a divorce or separation you've experienced? How was it different?**
- **By one of you leaving during this project, did it help you understand someone who's left you? If so, how?**

Have kids gather the index cards and hand them to you. Give each group paper and a pencil. Have someone in each group read aloud Ruth 1:1-18. Then have foursomes assign one of the following roles to each person in the group: Ruth, Orpah, Naomi, or Scribe. Say: **Answer the following questions as if you were your assigned character. For example, if you're Ruth, answer the questions as if you were her. Scribes, you're responsible for recording your group's answers and sharing them when we meet as a big group.**

Ask:

- **How did you feel when your husband died?**
- **What worries do you have about the future?**
- **If you could change anything about the recent events of your life, what would you change?**

When foursomes have finished, have the Scribes read their papers to

LEADER TIP for The Study

This study delves into the painful topics of divorce and abandonment. Many of your students, and perhaps some of your adult leaders, will be confronted with feelings they'd rather avoid: sadness, loneliness, guilt, or anger. Prepare for this study by praying with your adult leaders for your students and for themselves.

During the study, create an environment that allows kids to express their feelings but doesn't force them to share more than they're willing. They may wish to leave your meeting to avoid pain. Appoint one or two adult leaders to check on these students and talk with them about their feelings. Be available to your students after class; they may be more willing to share if they can talk to you one-on-one.

Call these kids during the week to assess how well they're processing their feelings. If they've uncovered some unbearably painful memories or feelings, refer them to a professional counselor or therapist you trust.

the whole class. Then have foursomes discuss this question:

- **How are Naomi's, Orpah's, and Ruth's feelings like how you felt when your parents divorced, a friend's parents divorced, or someone abandoned you in another way?**

Read aloud Matthew 27:45-50 and John 16:32-33. Have foursomes answer these questions:

- **What do these passages say about Jesus' experience with abandonment?**
- **How are Jesus' feelings similar to yours? How are they different?**
- **What's it like to know Jesus experienced the pain of abandonment, too?**

Say: **Jesus knows exactly how you feel when you've been abandoned. But he experienced abandonment that you'll never have to feel—abandonment by God. Because Jesus suffered the pain of that intense separation, God is with you when you hurt.**

3 REFLECTION ▼

> **LEADER TIP for Being There**
>
> If no one places a card outside both circles, ask kids what kinds of experiences might make them feel that no one was there for them. As kids volunteer situations, write each one on a separate card, and scatter the cards outside the circles.

Being There (10 to 15 minutes)

Say: **Think again about times you've felt abandoned. In this next experience, we're going to discover who's been there for us in the middle of our pain.**

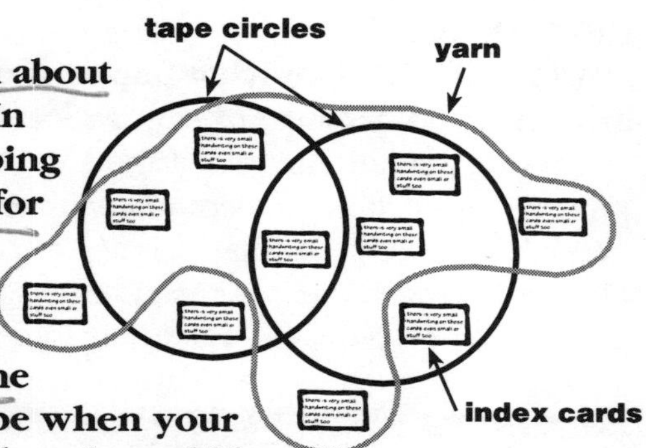

Give each student an index card and a pencil. Say: **On the card I gave you, write one time you felt abandoned. It could be when your parents separated or divorced, or it could be when a friend moved away. If you wish to write more than one situation, you may get more index cards from me. Don't write your name on your cards.**

While kids write their situations, use masking tape to make two circles, each four feet wide, on the floor. Make sure the circles intersect. When you've finished, say: **The left circle represents "my family was there for me" and the right circle represents "my friends were there for me." The intersection represents "my family and my friends were there for me." Outside the circles represents "no one was there for me." Look at the situation you wrote on your card, then place your card face up inside or outside the circles that best represent who was there for you during that situation. If no one was there for you, you may place your card as far away from the circles as you felt from other people.**

Have kids form a circle around the scattered cards. Say: **Together we've created a picture of the support we did or didn't feel when going through tough times. Read all the cards on the floor. In relation to the situations on the cards, where would you draw a "God was there for me" circle? We're going to create such a circle now.**

I'm going to pass a ball of yarn around the circle. When the yarn comes to you, bend down and lay the yarn around the cards on the floor in front of you. If you think God would be with you in a situation written on a card, lay the yarn so that card is inside the circle. If you think God wouldn't be with you in that situation, lay the yarn so the card is outside the circle. When you've created your part of the yarn circle, pass the yarn to the person next to you.

Pass a ball of yarn around the circle, keeping one end of the yarn in your hand. When everyone has finished creating his or her part of the yarn circle, put your end of the yarn down to complete the circle. Then have everyone look at the circle. If the group put some of the cards outside the "God was there for me" circle, have kids discuss why they believe God wouldn't be with them in those situations. During this discussion, kids may change their minds about whether God would be with them. If they do, allow kids to change the yarn circle to include or exclude those situations.

Have volunteers read aloud Psalm 145:17-20; Matthew 28:20; John 16:32-33; and Hebrews 4:16. Say: **These verses say that God is with you when you hurt. That means that God will see you through every painful situation you could ever experience. If your parents divorce or if you feel abandoned for any other reason, God is with you. The yarn circle we've created represents times God was with us. Since God is always with us, let's make sure that our "God was there for me" circle includes every single card.** If the yarn doesn't already encircle all of the cards, have kids move the yarn to include all the cards in the circle. Then have kids stand inside that circle and spend a few moments in prayer, thanking God for being with them when they hurt, and asking God to make his comfort real to them in times of need.

LEADER TIP for The Study

Allow kids to form groups with their friends. Your students will probably feel more comfortable expressing their feelings if they're with people they trust.

DEPTHFINDER — UNDERSTANDING THESE KIDS

It's really easy to judge divorced families. God speaks clearly against divorce in the Bible, except in the cases of adultery (Matthew 5:31-32) and abandonment by an unbelieving spouse (1 Corinthians 7:10-16). In Mark 10:2-12, Jesus made it clear that God created marriage so that two people would become one, never to separate. In Malachi 2:14-16, we learn that God hates divorce.

Despite what God's Word says, divorce happens frequently in our country, and kids experience the hurt and shame that comes with it. If your students know how God truly feels about divorce, they may bear the guilt for their parents' choices. Many kids believe they caused their parents' divorces. The tapes run in their minds: "If only I'd been more obedient," "If only I'd gotten better grades," "If only my sister and I had gotten along better." Because of their perceived part in the divorce, these kids may fear that God will abandon them.

In these painful times, your kids need to know that God will always be with them. Encourage your kids to read passages about God's nearness, such as Psalm 145:17-20. And be an envoy of God's nearness by being available for your kids when they need encouragement or a listening ear.

pairs
↳ same as last wk

COMMITMENT TIME ▼

I'm Here

(10 to 15 minutes)

Have kids form trios and read Psalm 145:17-20.

Say: **God is with you when you hurt. In your trios, tell each other at least one way God has been with you when you've hurt. For example, perhaps God brought a new friend into your life when your parents were divorcing or when you felt abandoned.**

When trios have finished, say: **When we feel abandoned, it's nice to hear something positive about ourselves. In your trios, take turns completing the following sentence: "You're worth sticking around for because . . ." For example, you could say, "You're worth sticking around for because you listen when others feel hurt."**

As kids encourage each other, give each trio three copies of the "Being There" handout (p. 33) and pencils. Encourage trios to fill out the information on the handouts, cut them out, put them in their wallets or something they always carry with them, and follow the guidelines on the handouts whenever they feel abandoned.

handout

being THERE | being THERE | being THERE

1. When you need a friend, call your partners and meet with them.

Name: ______________________ Phone #: ______________________

Name: ______________________ Phone #: ______________________

2. When you meet, spend a moment in prayer together. Ask God to be with you as you help each other.

3. Tell your friends what you're feeling.

4. Ask your friends for ideas on how to handle the hurt.

5. Read one or more of the following Scriptures: Psalm 145:17-20; Matthew 28:20; John 16:32-33; and Hebrews 4:16.

6. Talk about how these passages apply to your situation.

7. Pray again, asking God to comfort you and give you confidence in the middle of the pain.

8. Trust God to be with you.

1. When you need a friend, call your partners and meet with them.

Name: ______________________ Phone #: ______________________

Name: ______________________ Phone #: ______________________

2. When you meet, spend a moment in prayer together. Ask God to be with you as you help each other.

3. Tell your friends what you're feeling.

4. Ask your friends for ideas on how to handle the hurt.

5. Read one or more of the following Scriptures: Psalm 145:17-20; Matthew 28:20; John 16:32-33; and Hebrews 4:16.

6. Talk about how these passages apply to your situation.

7. Pray again, asking God to comfort you and give you confidence in the middle of the pain.

8. Trust God to be with you.

Bridging the Poverty Gap

helping those in less fortunate circumstances

by Lisa Baba Lauffer

THE POINT:

You can bring hope to the hurting.

■ The numbers are astounding. ■ Fifteen percent of Americans live below the poverty line. That category includes one of every three blacks and almost one in every three Hispanics. Almost fifteen million children—22 percent of all children in America—live in poverty. (Michael Gartner, "Put Christmas spirit into action," USA Today, Dec. 19, 1995.) ■ God told us that there would always be poor people in the world and that those more fortunate would need to take care of them—that he'd provide for the poor through those who have more than enough. And that's not just in terms of physical needs, such as food, clothing, and shelter. God knew that some of us would be emotionally drained, unable to help ourselves through our problems, or spiritually impoverished, our lives completely devoid of meaning. ■ And God gave us enough resources to help each other through our suffering.

The Study AT A GLANCE

SECTION	MINUTES	WHAT STUDENTS WILL DO	SUPPLIES
Economic Resource Simulation	15 to 20	**WALL OF DREAMS**—Create a Wall of Dreams and attempt to reach it by "climbing" a Ladder of Success based on the number of beans they possess.	Newsprint, masking tape, markers, dry beans, small plastic bags
	5 to 10	**POVERTY IS . . .**—Create a definition of poverty for reference during the rest of the study.	Newsprint, tape, marker
Bible Exploration	15 to 20	**POVERTY IN THE BIBLE**—Explore Bible passages about helping those in poverty.	Bibles, "Helping the Poor" handouts (p. 45), pencils
Choosing a Response	10 to 15	**OPEN HANDS**—Try to gather candy bars with their fists clenched.	Candy bars with paper wrappers, stopwatch, ballpoint pens

notes:

notes : need --

- "jelly beans" / something 2 keep count with
- marks 4 level on rung (step "stairs"?)
- paper across 7 wall - 4 dreams
- permanent marker?
- chocolates per person
- photostate worksheet

THE POINT OF *BRIDGING THE POVERTY GAP:*

You can bring hope to the hurting.

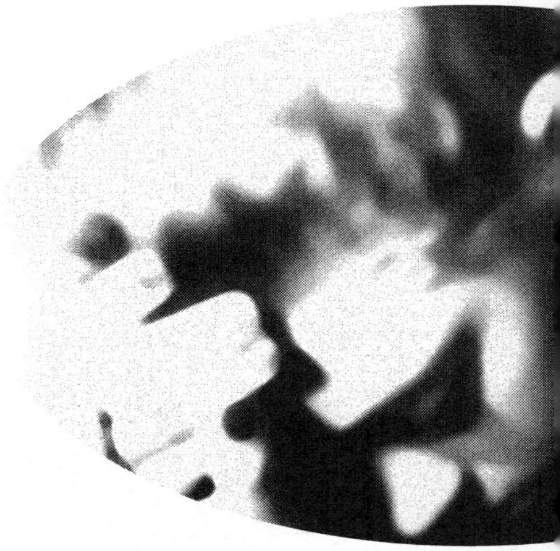

THE BIBLE CONNECTION

DEUTERONOMY 15:1-11	God proclaims that there will always be poor people in the world.
PROVERBS 19:17	Solomon explains that being kind to the poor is like lending to the Lord.
MATTHEW 5:3	Jesus preaches that those who know their spiritual needs are blessed.
2 CORINTHIANS 8:8-15	Paul encourages us to give to each other so everyone can be equal.

In this study, kids will play a poverty "game" where they'll experience having different levels of resources than those around them. Then they'll explore Bible passages about helping those who experience material, emotional, and spiritual poverty.

Through this experience, your young people can broaden their views on poverty and discover how to fulfill God's imperative to take care of the materially, emotionally, and spiritually poor.

LEADER TIP for The Study

Whenever groups discuss a list of questions, write the questions on newsprint, and tape the newsprint to the wall so groups can discuss the questions at their own pace.

BEFORE THE STUDY

Cover one wall of your meeting room with newsprint. Then between the wall with the newsprint and the opposite wall, tape six masking tape lines parallel to the walls and to each other. Make the lines extend to the walls perpendicular to them. (See the diagram below.)

Then gather enough small plastic bags for each student to have one. In one out of every six bags, place two beans. Then in one out of every five of the remaining bags, place sixteen beans. In each of the remaining bags, place eight beans.

Wall of Dreams

THE STUDY

ECONOMIC RESOURCE SIMULATION ▼

(15 to 20 minutes)

Wall of Dreams As kids arrive, have them write on the newsprint some realistic dreams they have for the future. If they wish, have students draw pictures representing these dreams. Allow kids to be as specific or vague as they wish. Encourage them to think of categories such as marriage, family, job, hobbies, travel, friends, and home ownership.

After everyone has arrived and written for about three minutes, have kids form a line along the wall opposite from the newsprint-covered wall. Have them stand facing the newsprint. Hand each student one of the bean-filled plastic bags you prepared before the study. Go down the line, giving out the two-bean bags, the eight-bean bags, then the sixteen-bean bags. Have kids remain in line and number off by fours. This should "spread the wealth" among counted-off number groups.

LEADER TIP for The Study

Because this topic can be so powerful and relevant to kids' lives, your group members may be tempted to get caught up in issues and lose sight of the deeper biblical principle found in The Point. Help your kids grasp The Point by guiding them to focus on the biblical investigation and discussing how God's truth connects with reality in their lives.

DEPTHFINDER — UNDERSTANDING POVERTY

According to Marvin Olasky in USA Today, poverty isn't just a material matter. Olasky says:

Some people are poor through no fault of their own, but others are impoverished because of spiritual problems that manifest themselves in addiction, alcoholism, family abandonment, promiscuity, laziness or crime.

Those troubled poor have holes in their souls that only God can fill.

It's not that the rich have fewer spiritual holes than the poor, but rather that the former are better able to plug those holes with putty, temporarily.

Recognition of spiritual need should not lead the better-off to scorn the troubled poor, but rather to offer effective compassion that is challenging, personal and spiritual.

(Marvin Olasky is a senior fellow at the Progress and Freedom Foundation and co-founder of the Center for Effective Compassion. Quote is from his article "Holes in the soul matter as much as dollars," USA Today, Feb. 15, 1996.)

Whenever we reach out to those less fortunate, we need to look beyond the physical circumstances and emotional causes to the spiritual needs that those in poverty have. We all have voids in our hearts that only God can fill—it's just that some who are better off fill the void temporarily and dull the ache with material things. Encourage your young people to look beyond both material poverty and material wealth to see hurting, needy people. Those in poverty can be filled and begin the road to recovery by trusting their lives to Jesus Christ, who offers them treasure that is priceless—eternal life.

Say: **We all hope to meet our dreams someday. But for some people, perhaps even some of you in this room, circumstances make reaching our dreams difficult. We're going to play a game to illustrate this.**

The goal of our game is to reach the Wall of Dreams you just created. I'll describe a number of circumstances, and you can advance toward the wall as I direct based on the number of beans you have. You advance by "climbing" the Ladder of Success taped to the floor. There will be opportunities for you to earn and lose beans as the game progresses. This will happen according to your counted-off number (one through four), so remember your number. The person to reach the Wall of Dreams first, possessing the greatest number of beans will be our winner.

To start the game, step onto the first "rung" of our Ladder of Success. To do so, you must possess at least four beans.

Allow kids time to get on the ladder. The kids who have only two beans will not be able to climb the ladder and will most likely complain. Just tell them that you're playing by the rules of the game and proceed.

Then read aloud the information in the table on page 40, reading the entries in each row from left to right. After reading each row, give beans to or take beans from kids as designated in the table. Also allow kids to proceed on the Ladder of Success as directed in the table.

When one or more students reach the Wall of Dreams, figure out who got there with the most beans and congratulate them. Then have kids form groups of four with each group having a One, Two, Three, and Four in it. Ask:

- **What's your reaction to this game?**
- **How fair did you think this game was? Explain.**
- **How did you feel knowing that some people had been excluded from the game based on the number of beans they possessed?**
- **Some of you had enough beans to give to those who didn't have enough to play. Did you do that? Why or why not?**
- **How do you feel knowing that everyone could have played the game if some people had shared their beans with others?**
- **How might your experience in this game be like people's experience in real life?**

Say: **One of every six of you had only two beans, were unable to participate in our game, and thus had no chance of winning. In our society, almost one of every six people lives in poverty without much chance of reaching the dreams we've portrayed on our Wall of Dreams.**

Today we're going to discuss poverty. When we talk about poverty, we most often refer to material poverty—the lack of food, shelter, clothing, and other material things that most people in our society are used to having. But there are other kinds of poverty such as emotional poverty and spiritual poverty. Whatever kind of poverty people experience, <u>you can bring hope to the hurting.</u>

POINT

Collect the beans from the students before moving to the next section.

LEADER TIP for Wall of Dreams

To make this game go smoothly, recruit an adult volunteer to hand out beans according to your instructions. This way you don't have to stop the game to hand out beans yourself.

LEADER TIP for Wall of Dreams

This game is designed to illustrate the proportions of people who live in poverty, which is a statistic of approximately one in six. However, if you have fewer than six students participating in this study, you can still play the game to illustrate the cyclical forces that keep people in impoverished circumstances. To do this, make sure you give one student two beans, another student sixteen beans, and the rest eight beans.

Also in this game, students number off by fours. Through the experience, different things will happen to people with different numbers. This creates a way to simulate somewhat random events so kids can understand how one's economic resources impact a person's ability to succeed in the face of these events. To facilitate this in smaller groups, have students number off by fours if possible.

Table For "Wall of Dreams"

EVENTS OF LIFE	BEANS EXCHANGED	STEPS ON LADDER OF SUCCESS
High school graduation: • *Ones* don't graduate. • *Everyone else* does. • *Fours* are at the head of the class and receive scholarships.	• *Fours* receive two "scholarship" beans.	• *Ones* stay put through entire game. • *Everyone else* moves forward one rung.
Decisions to attend college: • *Everyone with seven or more beans* goes to college and can afford to do so either by their own means or through scholarships.		• *Everyone with seven or more beans* moves forward one rung.
College graduation: • *Threes* with eleven or fewer beans drop out of college. • *Threes* with twelve or more beans struggle but graduate because they pay tutors to help them. • *Everyone else* on this rung graduates.	• *Threes* with twelve or more beans pay two beans.	• *Everyone on this rung* moves forward one rung *except the Threes with eleven or fewer beans.*
Getting jobs: • *People with seven or fewer beans* get jobs at minimum wage. • *People with eight to fourteen beans* get entry-level professional jobs, unless they dropped out of college in which case they get a minimum wage job. • *People with fifteen or more beans* move right into a professional job that is waiting just for them.	• *People with seven or fewer beans* receive one bean. • *People with eight to fourteen beans* receive two beans, *unless they dropped out of college* in which case they receive only one bean. • *People with fifteen to eighteen beans* receive two beans.	• *People with fourteen or fewer beans* move forward one rung. • *People with fifteen or more beans* move forward two rungs.
Buying a house: • *People with twelve or more beans* buy houses.	• *People with twelve or more beans* pay two beans.	• *People with twelve or more beans* move forward one rung.

Poverty Is... (5 to 10 minutes)

Ask:

- **What does the word "poverty" mean to you?**
- **What do the terms "emotional poverty" and "spiritual poverty" mean to you?**

Tape a fresh sheet of newsprint to a wall, and on it write kids' responses to the two questions. Then have the group develop a definition of poverty that encompasses material, emotional, and spiritual poverty. For example, kids might agree on a definition similar to one in Webster's New World Dictionary: "a lack of the resources for reasonably comfortable living." Write the group's definition on a new sheet of newsprint, and post the newsprint where everyone can see it during the study.

LEADER TIP for Wall of Dreams

If no one has reached the Wall of Dreams by the time you've finished reading through the table, say that the Fours each have inherited money from wealthy grandparents. Give each Four two beans, and allow them to move forward until you have a winner.

I am not commanding you to give. But I want to see if your love is true by comparing you with others that really want to help. You know the grace of our Lord Jesus Christ. You know that Christ was rich, but for you he became poor so that by his becoming poor you might become rich.

This is what I think you should do: Last year you were the first who gave. So now finish the work you started. Then your "doing" will be equal to your "wanting to do." Give from what you have. If you want to give, your gift will be accepted.

2 Corinthians 8:8-12a

Say: **During our activities and discussions today, this definition will be our point of reference. We're going to explore the subject of poverty further, especially looking at what the Bible says about it. As we do, you'll discover that <u>you can bring hope to the hurting.</u>**

BIBLE EXPLORATION ▼

> **LEADER TIP for Poverty in the Bible**
>
> If each of the three groups has more than five students, have students within each group find partners and go through the handout as pairs.

Poverty in the Bible (15 to 20 minutes)

Give each student a copy of the "Helping the Poor" handout (p. 45), then have students form three groups. Assign each group one of the following categories of poverty: material, emotional, and spiritual. Then assign each group its respective Scripture passage: 2 Kings 4:1-7 (material poverty); John 11:17-37 (emotional poverty); and John 4:1-30 (spiritual poverty). Have each group go through the handout according to its assigned poverty category.

After poverty groups finish their discussions, have kids form trios made up of one student from each group. Then have students explain in their trios what they learned about their particular poverty categories and list ways to help those experiencing the different types of poverty. Then have each person tell one way he or she will bring hope to someone who is hurting. For example, kids could choose to make and send a homemade card to someone who has recently experienced the loss of a friend (emotional poverty) or tell someone about Jesus' gift of eternal life (spiritual poverty).

After everyone has shared, have each trio member describe a positive characteristic about the person on his or her right that will help that person bring hope to the hurting. For example, students could say something such as "You can bring hope to the hurting because you focus on the positive in almost every situation." Then have trios pray for God to help them bring hope to the hurting.

When trios have finished praying, say: **<u>You can bring hope to the hurting.</u> It doesn't matter what resources you have. Maybe you don't have as much money as someone else, but you have joy to share with others. We all have something to give, whether it's a possession or encouragement or knowledge of Jesus Christ. I challenge you to think of ways you can give to others, to bring hope to those who need it.**

CHOOSING A RESPONSE ▼

Open Hands (10 to 15 minutes)

Say: **We're going to participate in one more experience to remember how <u>you can bring hope to the hurting.</u>**

DEPTH FINDER

WHAT HAPPENS WHEN KIDS HELP

Do you want to give your kids an opportunity to help those less fortunate than they? Consider bringing your young people to a Group workcamp! Every summer thousands of students help build, paint, and repair houses for the disadvantaged and elderly. But the people who receive the help aren't the only ones who benefit. According to Thom Schultz in "Helping Kids Become Servants" (GROUP Magazine, January 1993, from Group's MinistryNet™), when young people have the opportunity to serve, they receive intangible rewards that are priceless. Kids' faith becomes real, their self-esteem grows, and they learn to serve as a lifestyle.

If you're interested in providing your young people this type of opportunity, call Group Workcamps at 1-800-774-3838, and inquire about the junior/senior high workcamps available.

Have kids form a circle. Then have kids make fists. Set a pile of candy bars in front of one student. Choose candy bars with paper wrappers such as Hershey's chocolate bars. Make sure you have enough candy bars so each student can have one.

Say: **The object of our game is to pass the candy bars around the circle so each person has one. But you must keep your hands in fists. I'm going to time you to see how fast you can do this.** Tell the person with the pile of candy bars that he or she is the start person.

When everyone understands the game, tell them to begin. Then start your stopwatch. When everyone has a candy bar, stop your stopwatch and announce the time. Collect the candy bars and repeat the game, this time allowing kids to open their hands to pass the candy bars. When everyone has a candy bar, stop your stopwatch and announce the time.

Ask:

- **Which is easier: picking up candy bars with your hands clenched in fists or open? Explain.**
- **How is passing candy bars with clenched fists like the way we hold onto our possessions or our emotional or spiritual energy?**
- **How is passing candy bars with our hands open like freely giving away what we have to those less fortunate than us?**
- **How can you have an openhanded attitude toward people you know?**

Have kids find places for solitude. Hand out ballpoint pens, and encourage your students to eat their candy bars and then on the inside of their wrappers write prayers about their feelings on poverty. If they wish, have them write commitments to help people who are in poverty of any kind.

DEPTHFINDER

UNDERSTANDING VOLUNTEERING

According to Theresa Foy DiGeronimo in her book *A Student's Guide to Volunteering*, students who volunteer to help those less fortunate than they often have the following characteristics:

"They aren't judgmental toward those less fortunate than themselves.

They are responsible and committed.

They are compassionate and concerned for the welfare of others.

They follow orders well.

They can deal with meeting people who have not bathed, are poorly clothed, or are suffering.

They are team players."

Most of these characteristics apply whether kids are helping those experiencing material, emotional, or spiritual poverty. Encourage your students to develop these characteristics and to put them into practice with those around them, such as people at school who come from lower-income neighborhoods, those who struggle with depression, or those who have never heard of Jesus Christ before.

helping the poor

ASSIGNED POVERTY CATEGORY: ______________________________

ASSIGNED SCRIPTURE PASSAGE: ______________________________

READ YOUR ASSIGNED SCRIPTURE PASSAGE, AND ANSWER THE FOLLOWING QUESTIONS:

- Who in your passage experienced the kind of poverty you're studying? How?

- Who helped that person? How?

- How did that person's help bring hope to someone who was hurting?

READ THE FOLLOWING PASSAGES. UNDER EACH PASSAGE, WRITE WHAT EACH PASSAGE COMMUNICATES ABOUT HELPING PEOPLE IN POVERTY AND HOW THAT PASSAGE SPECIFICALLY APPLIES TO YOUR ASSIGNED CATEGORY OF POVERTY.

- Deuteronomy 15:1-11

- Proverbs 19:17

- Matthew 5:3

- 2 Corinthians 8:8-15

NOW ANSWER THESE QUESTIONS:

- How can you tell when someone is experiencing your assigned category of poverty?

- What are some ways you can help people in your category of poverty?

The Grand Scheme

Searching for God's Perspective on Disappointment

Searching for God's Perspective on Disappointment

by Karl Leuthauser

THE POINT:

God brings good out of suffering.

■ "If I were in charge, things would be different. Parents would have to stay married, oversize jerks wouldn't get away with shoving the trumpet player into his locker, tests would always cover what we learned in class, and boys wouldn't date girls just because they show off their bodies." ■ Your kids are constantly challenged with disappointment. Whether it's found in wavering friends, unstable family, unjust authority, or unrealistic expectations, disappointment hurts. Kids come to the end of their abilities and in frustration and humiliation ask, "Why me?" ■ It's tempting to give pat answers, to encourage kids to put on a smile until junior high is over, and to tell them that in ten years they'll barely remember the disappointments they will have faced in school. The Bible, however, doesn't tell us to ignore or downplay pain. It encourages us to endure pain, to make the most of it, and to know that God is in control.

The Study
AT A GLANCE

SECTION	MINUTES	WHAT STUDENTS WILL DO	SUPPLIES
Emotional Connection	10 to 15	GLOBAL DOMINION—Play a game in which they try to gain control over a giant grid in order to win a candy bar.	Bibles, tape, paper, newsprint, markers, "Rules for Global Dominion" handouts (p. 55), candy bar
	5 to 10	ROUND 2—Play a second round of Global Dominion in which everyone receives a candy bar.	Bibles, candy bars, paper and newsprint from "Global Dominion" activity
Creative Options	20 to 25	JUST LIKE JOSEPH—Look at the disappointments Joseph faced and present the lesson through creative options.	Bibles, paper, pencils, newsprint, tape, copies of the activity options
Personal Application	10 to 15	BRINGING IT HOME—Brainstorm about positive ways to deal with disappointment and apply them to personal situations.	Paper, markers

notes:

THE POINT OF *THE GRAND SCHEME:*

God brings good out of suffering.

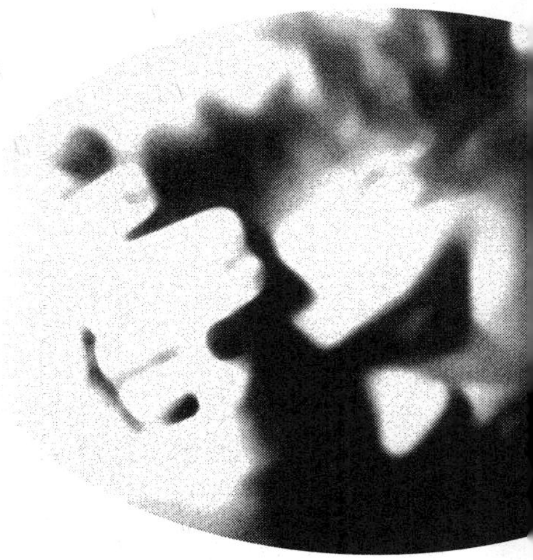

THE BIBLE CONNECTION

GENESIS 37:18-28; 39:7-23; 50:15-21	These verses explain a few of the disappointments Joseph faced and his reaction to those disappointments.
ISAIAH 55:8-9	These verses explain that God's perspective is higher than ours.
PSALM 120:1; ROMANS 12:12; JAMES 1:2-4; 5:13-18	These verses tell us how we should react when facing troubles.

In this study, kids will play a game in which they attempt to control a giant grid to help them understand that God knows what he's doing. By looking at the life of Joseph and presenting his story through creative options, they can discover the Bible's instructions on pain and disappointment. As they investigate ways to deal with personal disappointments, they can find that they have no reason for despair.

Explore the verses in The Bible Connection, then examine the information in the Depthfinder boxes throughout the study to gain a deeper understanding of how these Scriptures connect with your young people.

LEADER TIP for The Study

Whenever groups discuss a list of questions, write the list on newsprint and tape it to a wall so groups can discuss the questions at their own pace.

BEFORE THE STUDY

Use tape to divide the room into a grid of sixteen squares. Write the numerals one through sixteen on separate sheets of paper. Write the numerals one through sixteen on a sheet of newsprint, and tape the newsprint to the wall. Place a stack of paper and a few markers in the middle of the room.

Write each of the following activity options on a separate sheet of paper:

- Write a letter to God from Joseph that explains the difficulties he's having and the way he feels.
- Pretend that you're a nose hair that Joseph has had since junior high and you're talking to a nose hair that has just sprouted. Explain to the little kipper about the difficulties Joseph has faced. Include how it affected your life.
- Write a poem that Joseph may have written while in prison.
- Use the tune from the *Beverly Hillbillies* to create a song that describes the disappointments Joseph faced.

Make three copies of each of these activity options.

THE STUDY

EMOTIONAL CONNECTION ▼

Global Dominion

(10 to 15 minutes)

As kids arrive, distribute one numbered sheet of paper to each student. Say: **Please write your name next to the number on the sheet of newsprint that corresponds with the number I have given you. For example, if you have a sheet with number eight, write your name next to the eight on the newsprint. Then duplicate your number on fifteen separate sheets of paper.**

When they finish, say: **We're about to play a game of Global Dominion. The winner of the game will receive a candy bar as well as the glory that comes with being the supreme dictator of the world.** Distribute the "Rules for Global Dominion" handouts, (p. 55) and ask the kids to follow along as you read the rules.

Have your students take turns placing their numbers in the squares. Begin with the student that has the number one, then have the other students take turns in numerical order. When all the squares have been filled, ask if anyone has questions about the rules. After you answer questions, have the students take turns attacking other squares. Use the sheet of newsprint with the numbers and names to help you keep the correct order.

Give the candy bar to the winner, and ask the students to set aside their numbers for later use. Be sure everyone has a Bible and have kids form groups of four to discuss the following questions:

LEADER TIP for Global Dominion

If you have sixteen or more participants in the Global Dominion activity, add a square to the grid for each additional student. Prepare one numbered sheet and one number on the newsprint for each student. Be sure students duplicate their numbers so they have one sheet for each square on the grid. Have students stand in the squares and exchange numbers according to the outcome of the battles instead of placing their numbers in the empty squares. Have the person that is attacking another square direct one of his or her conquered subjects to fight the battle if the attacker isn't standing next to the square he or she is attacking.

DEPTHFINDER — UNDERSTANDING YOUR KIDS

You may wonder why your kids perseverate on insignificant and juvenile disappointments. Part of the reason is found in the limited perspective that teenagers can have. For instance, it's difficult for them to understand that the dating scene will pan out when they've just entered the game. Their inability to deal with trying times may also have something to do with overwhelming difficulties they've already faced. After dealing with divorce, abuse, and poor role models, kids see minor setbacks as insurmountable disappointments because they've been shaken and challenged at their very core.

As a youth leader, you can help your kids cope with the important and insignificant disappointments they face. You can remind them that they can make it; you can actively listen to their plight; you can refer them to a professional counselor; and you can help them find their options. Your perspective of a few more or many more years may be the difference that keeps your kids alive.

- **How much control did you have over the outcome of the game?**
- **How important was it to you to win the game? Why?**
- **Were you disappointed when your number was completely destroyed? Why or why not?**
- **If all the participants had more control over the outcome of the game, do you think it would be more or less important for you to win? Why?**
- **Think of a disappointing circumstance you've been through. Did you have control over what happened? Explain.**
- **Would the outcome of your circumstance have been different if you had more control of the situation? If so, how?**
- **Read James 1:2-4. What do these verses tell us to do when we face disappointments that are out of our control? Why do you think God instructs us to do this?**

Call the kids back together, and ask a volunteer to read aloud Romans 12:12. Then say: **Most of the disappointments that we face are the results of things that are out of our control. We want certain things to happen or to go a certain way, and when they don't, we feel disappointed. It's not wrong to hope for certain things to happen. But when they don't, we need to be patient because <u>God brings good out of suffering.</u> Let me show you what I mean.**

Round 2 (5 to 10 minutes)

Ask the students to pick up their numbers from the Global Dominion activity. Say: **We're going to play another round of Global Dominion. The winner of the round will receive a candy bar.** Have kids play the game exactly as they did in the Global Dominion activity. Congratulate the winner and give him or her a candy bar. Leave the grid on the floor and have kids set aside their numbers for later use.

Ask: **Was anyone who lost the game disappointed that he or she didn't get a candy bar?** Toss candy bars to those who say they were disappointed. If not everyone responds, ask: **Would anyone else like a candy bar?** Toss candy bars to those who respond.

Have a volunteer read Isaiah 55:8-9. Then say: **After the second round of Global Dominion, everyone had the opportunity to receive a candy bar, but before you knew that, you may have been disappointed that you didn't receive one. It turned out that everyone who wanted a candy bar got one. They just had to wait for a little while. I'm not saying that God will give you whatever you want if you just wait long enough, but he does want us to be patient when we face disappointment because his perspective is different from ours. He knows the outcome of all the situations that we face. We can have hope through disappointing times because <u>God brings good out of suffering.</u> He knows the end result of our disappointing circumstances, and he can use them for his good.**

Have students get in pairs and share a disappointment that they are dealing with. Ask the kids to help each other see the circumstance from a different perspective by explaining how they have already seen God working out his plan in their lives.

LEADER TIP for Global Dominion

To make the activity easier on the environment and your budget, use discarded paper from an office or from your home. Throw the paper in a recycling bin after the activity.

CREATIVE OPTIONS ▼

Just Like Joseph

(20 to 25 minutes)

Randomly place all of the activity options you prepared before the study face down in the sixteen squares from the Global Dominion activity. Write "Genesis 37:18-28; 39:7-23" on a sheet of newsprint, and tape it to the wall.

Say: **We're going to take some time to look at a few of the disappointments that Joseph faced. All of these sheets of paper on the floor have various options that explain how you can present to the rest of the group what you discover about Joseph. Each group should pick a representative to choose one of the options. Decide who is going to pick the option for your group.**

Have the representatives pick one of the sixteen sheets of paper. Then say: **I'd like your group to read the Bible verses listed on the newsprint and prepare to present what you discovered to the rest of the group.** Give kids about ten minutes to read and prepare. After all the groups have presented their options have groups discuss the following questions:

- **How do you think Joseph felt about God while he was in prison? about his family?**
- **If you were in Joseph's situation, how would you react to your family when you saw them again?**
- **How do you usually react to disappointment?**
- **What's the best way to react to disappointment?**

Call kids back together, and say: **As some of you may know,**

DEPTHFINDER

UNDERSTANDING THE BIBLE

Paul faced more than his share of disappointments. In 2 Corinthians 11:23-30, Paul describes some of the suffering he faced. He had received thirty-nine lashes with a whip on five separate occasions from the very people he was attempting to reach with the gospel. He was beaten with rods three times and was almost stoned to death. He was involved in three shipwrecks, and during one of those shipwrecks, he spent all day and night at sea. He had gone without sleep, food, and water. The book of Acts relates that he was put in prison for two years by the Judean governor Felix (23:1–26:32) and was later placed under house arrest in Rome for another two years (28:16-31). It is probable that Paul was arrested four years after his release in Rome and was executed at the hands of Nero.

Despite all these disappointments, Paul explains in Philippians 4:12b that he has "learned the secret of being content in every situation" (NIV). Perhaps the secret has something to do with his understanding of God's nature and God's purpose for his life. This sense of understanding is found in 2 Corinthians 4:8-9, in which Paul writes: "We have troubles all around us, but we are not defeated. We do not know what to do, but we do not give up the hope of living. We are persecuted, but God does not leave us. We are hurt sometimes, but we are not destroyed. We carry the death of Jesus in our own bodies so that the life of Jesus can also be seen in our bodies."

read

Joseph was released from prison and was made the second most powerful man in Egypt because God helped him to interpret a dream that the king of Egypt had. God used Joseph to set up a huge supply of food for a famine that was about to occur. He saw his brothers again, but at that time he had the power to do whatever he wanted to do to them. Let's look at Joseph's response.

Have a volunteer read Genesis 50:15-21. Then say: **Joseph understood that God brings good out of suffering. Joseph saw how God took the disappointments that he faced and used them for good. He could've sought revenge; he could've complained; he could've given his brothers the silent treatment. Instead, he chose to show them kindness.**

LEADER TIP for The Study

Because this topic can be so powerful and relevant to kids' lives, your group members may be tempted to get caught up in issues and lose sight of the deeper biblical principle found in The Point. Help your kids grasp The Point by guiding kids to focus on the biblical investigation and discussing how God's truth connects with reality in their lives.

PERSONAL APPLICATION ▼

Bringing It Home

(10 to 15 minutes)

Ask the kids to clear the remaining paper from the squares used in the previous activities. While they work, write "Encouraging Others" on a sheet of paper. Then say: **It's helpful to know that God brings good out of suffering, but we still need to decide how to deal with it. Let's help each other do that by coming up with some good ways to deal with disappointment. After you've shared your idea, I'd like you to write it on a piece of paper, and place it face up in one of the squares. Let's see if we can fill all the squares with different positive ways to deal with disappointment.**

Before kids start sharing their ideas, hold up the "Encouraging Others" sheet, and say: **One way that I deal with disappointment is**

LEADER TIP for Bringing it Home

If your students have a difficult time coming up with ideas for dealing with disappointment, offer some suggestions. You may want to include the following: letting go of control, being patient, finding the good in the circumstances, thinking of ways to change the situation, praying, talking to a friend, taking action, trying again, or trying something else.

DEPTHFINDER — ACT, DON'T REACT

"When she could hide him no longer she got a papyrus basket for him, and plastered it with bitumen and pitch; she put the child in it and placed it among the reeds on the bank of the river" (Exodus 2:3, New Revised Standard Version).

Moses' mother knew how wrong it would be to destroy her child. But there was little she could do to change Pharaoh's new law. Her only alternative was to hide the child and later place him in a tiny reed basket on the river. God used her courageous act to place her son, the Hebrew of his choice, in the house of Pharaoh. Do you sometimes feel surrounded by evil and frustrated by how little you can do about it? When faced with evil, look for ways to act against it. Then trust God to use your effort, however small it seems, in his war against evil.

("Act, Don't React" excerpted from *The Student's A to Z Guide to Bible Application*, Tyndale House Publishers.)

LEADER TIP for The Study

Share the information from the "Act, Don't React" Depthfinder with your students. If you have additional time after working through the study, read and discuss the Depthfinder. If you don't have extra time, allow kids to read "Act, Don't React" on their own.

by encouraging others. Helping others helps me to keep from focusing on myself and the disappointments I face.

Encourage kids to offer ideas. When all the squares are filled or when the kids run out of ideas, say: **Think of one thing that has disappointed you or that's disappointing to you right now. Look at the positive ways we've come up with to deal with disappointment, and choose one or two appropriate ways to deal with your situation.**

Have kids get into pairs and pray for God's help with the disappointments that they face. Encourage them to ask God to give them the strength to deal with their disappointments in positive ways.

• sing 'Hungry"

Rules for Global Dominion

1. The object of the game is to take over the world.
2. You have successfully taken over the world if your number is in every square in the grid.
3. You must attack one square on your turn.
4. You must be next to a square to attack it. You may not attack a square that is at a diagonal from where you're attacking.
5. You may attack from any one square that has your number in it.
6. To attack another number, stand in the square you wish to attack from and face the square you wish to attack. The attacker and the defender must play Rock, Paper, Scissors. Rock beats scissors, scissors beat paper, paper beats rock. Whoever wins Rock, Paper, Scissors wins the battle.
7. The square of the loser and all connecting squares with the same number become the property of the winner. Show this by discarding the loser's numbers and replacing them with the winner's numbers (see the diagrams below).
8. Squares that only touch diagonally do not become property of the winner. Squares with the same number as the loser that do not touch at all also do not become property of the winner.
9. After you attack a square and change the numbers in the won or lost squares, your turn is over.

sample move 1

If number "**one**" attacked number "**two**" from this square and won,

→1	2	2	3
3	4	2	4
2	3	4	1
3	1	3	2

The result would look like this:

1	1	1	3
3	4	1	4
2	3	4	1
3	1	3	2

sample move 2

If number "**one**" attacked number "**two**" from this square and lost,

2	↓1	4	3
3	1	1	4
2	3	4	1
2	4	3	1

The result would look like this:

2	2	4	3
3	2	2	4
2	3	4	1
2	4	3	1

handout

ok to copy

why Active and Interactive Learning works with teenagers

Let's Start With the Big Picture

Think back to a major life lesson you've learned.

Got it? Now answer these questions:

- Did you learn your lesson from something you read?
- Did you learn it from something you heard?
- Did you learn it from something you experienced?

If you're like 99 percent of your peers, you answered "yes" only to the third question—you learned your life lesson from something you experienced.

This simple test illustrates the most convincing reason for using active and interactive learning with young people: People learn best through experience. Or to put it even more simply, people learn by doing.

Learning by doing is what active learning is all about. No more sitting quietly in chairs and listening to a speaker expound theories about God—that's passive learning. Active learning gets kids out of their chairs and into the experience of life. With active learning, kids get to *do* what they're studying. They *feel* the effects of the principles you teach. They *learn* by experiencing truth firsthand.

Active learning works because it recognizes three basic learning needs and uses them in concert to enable young people to make discoveries on their own and to find practical life applications for the truths they believe.

So what are these three basic learning needs?

1. Teenagers need action.
2. Teenagers need to think.
3. Teenagers need to talk.

Read on to find out exactly how these needs will be met by using the active and interactive learning techniques in Group's Core Belief Bible Study Series in your youth group.

1. Teenagers Need Action

Aircraft pilots know well the difference between passive and active learning. Their passive learning comes through listening to flight instructors and reading flight-instruction books. Their active learning comes through actually flying an airplane or flight simulator. Books and lectures may be helpful, but pilots really learn to fly by manipulating a plane's controls themselves.

We can help young people learn in a similar way. Though we may engage students passively in some reading and listening to teachers, their understanding and application of God's Word will really take off through simulated and real-life experiences.

Forms of active learning include simulation games; role-plays; service projects; experiments; research projects; group pantomimes; mock trials; construction projects; purposeful games; field trips; and, of course, the most powerful form of active learning—real-life experiences.

We can more fully explain active learning by exploring four of its characteristics:

- **Active learning is an adventure.** Passive learning is almost always predictable. Students sit passively while the teacher or speaker follows a planned outline or script.

In active learning, kids may learn lessons the teacher never envisioned. Because the leader trusts students to help create the learning experience, learners may venture into unforeseen discoveries. And often the teacher learns as much as the students.

- **Active learning is fun and captivating.** What are we communicating when we say, "OK, the fun's over—time to talk about God"? What's the hidden message? That joy is separate from God? And that learning is separate from joy?

What a shame.

Active learning is not joyless. One seventh-grader we interviewed clearly remembered her best Sunday school lesson: "Jesus was the light, and we went into a dark room and shut off the lights. We had a candle, and we learned that Jesus is the light and the dark can't shut off the light." That's active learning. Deena enjoyed the lesson. She had fun. And she learned.

Active learning intrigues people. Whether they find a foot-washing experience captivating or maybe a bit uncomfortable, they learn. And they learn on a level deeper than any work sheet or teacher's lecture could ever reach.

- **Active learning involves everyone.** Here the difference between passive and active learning becomes abundantly clear. It's like the difference between watching a football game on television and actually playing in the game.

The "trust walk" provides a good example of involving everyone in active learning. Half of the group members put on blindfolds; the other half serve as guides. The "blind" people trust the guides to lead them through the building or outdoors. The guides prevent the blind people from falling down stairs or tripping over rocks. Everyone needs to participate to learn the inherent lessons of trust, faith, doubt, fear, confidence, and servanthood. Passive spectators of this experience would learn little, but participants learn a great deal.

- **Active learning is focused through debriefing.** Activity simply for activity's sake doesn't usually result in good learning. Debriefing—evaluating an experience by discussing it in pairs or small groups—helps focus the experience and draw out its meaning. Debriefing helps sort and order the information students gather during the experience. It helps learners relate the recently experienced activity to their lives.

The process of debriefing is best started immediately after an experience. We use a three-step process in debriefing: reflection, interpretation, and application.

Reflection—This first step asks the students, "How did you feel?" Active-learning experiences typically evoke an emotional reaction, so it's appropriate to begin debriefing at that level.

Some people ask, "What do feelings have to do with education?" Feelings have everything to do with education. Think back again to that time in your life when you learned a big lesson. In all likelihood, strong feelings accompanied that lesson. Our emotions tend to cement things into our memories.

When you're debriefing, use open-ended questions to probe feelings. Avoid questions that can be answered with a "yes" or "no." Let your learners know that there are no wrong answers to these "feeling" questions. Everyone's feelings are valid.

Interpretation—The next step in the debriefing process asks, "What does this mean to you? How is this experience like or unlike some other aspect of your life?" Now you're asking people to identify a message or principle from the experience.

You want your learners to discover the message for themselves. So instead of telling students your answers, take the time to ask questions that encourage self-discovery. Use Scripture and discussion in pairs or small groups to explore how the actions and effects of the activity might translate to their lives.

Alert! Some of your people may interpret wonderful messages that you never intended. That's not failure! That's the Holy Spirit at work. God allows us to catch different glimpses of his kingdom even when we all look through the same glass.

Application—The final debriefing step asks, "What will you do about it?" This step moves learning into action. Your young people have shared a common experience. They've discovered a principle. Now they must create something new with what they've just experienced and interpreted. They must integrate the message into their lives.

The application stage of debriefing calls for a decision. Ask your students how they'll change, how they'll grow, what they'll do as a result of your time together.

2. Teenagers Need to Think

Today's students have been trained not to think. They aren't dumber than previous generations. We've simply conditioned them not to use their heads.

You see, we've trained our kids to respond with the simplistic answers they think the teacher wants to hear. Fill-in-the-blank student workbooks and teachers who ask dead-end questions such as "What's the capital of Delaware?" have produced kids and adults who have learned not to think.

And it doesn't just happen in junior high or high school. Our children are schooled very early not to think. Teachers attempt to help kids read with nonsensical fill-in-the-blank drills, word scrambles, and missing-letter puzzles.

Helping teenagers think requires a paradigm shift in how we teach. We need to plan for and set aside time for higher-order thinking and be willing to reduce our time spent on lower-order parroting. Group's Core Belief Bible Study Series is designed to help you do just that.

Thinking classrooms look quite different from traditional classrooms. In most church environments, the teacher does most of the talking and hopes that knowledge will transmit from his or her brain to the students'. In thinking settings, the teacher coaches students to ponder, wonder, imagine, and problem-solve.

3. Teenagers Need to Talk

Everyone knows that the person who learns the most in any class is the teacher. Explaining a concept to someone else is usually more helpful to the explainer than to the listener. So why not let the students do more teaching? That's one of the chief benefits of letting kids do the talking. This process is called interactive learning.

What is interactive learning? Interactive learning occurs when students discuss and work cooperatively in pairs or small groups.

Interactive learning encourages learners to work together. It honors the fact that students can learn from one another, not just from the teacher. Students work together in pairs or small groups to accomplish shared goals. They build together, discuss together, and present together. They teach each other and learn from one another. Success as a group is celebrated. Positive interdependence promotes individual and group learning.

Interactive learning not only helps people learn but also helps learners feel better about themselves and get along better with others. It accomplishes these things more effectively than the independent or competitive methods.

Here's a selection of interactive learning techniques that are used in Group's Core Belief Bible Study Series. With any of these models, leaders may assign students to specific partners or small groups. This will maximize cooperation and learning by preventing all the "rowdies" from linking up. And it will allow for new friendships to form outside of established cliques.

Following any period of partner or small-group work, the leader may reconvene the entire class for large-group processing. During this time the teacher may ask for reports or discoveries from individuals or teams. This technique builds in accountability for the teacherless pairs and small groups.

Pair-Share—With this technique each student turns to a partner and responds to a question or problem from the teacher or leader. Every learner responds. There are no passive observers. The teacher may then ask people to share their partners' responses.

Study Partners—Most curricula and most teachers call for Scripture passages to be read to the whole class by one person. One reads; the others doze.

Why not relinquish some teacher control and let partners read and react with each other? They'll all be involved—and will learn more.

Learning Groups—Students work together in small groups to create a model, design artwork, or study a passage or story; then they discuss what they learned through the experience. Each person in the learning group may be assigned a specific role. Here are some examples:

Reader

Recorder (makes notes of key thoughts expressed during the reading or discussion)

Checker (makes sure everyone understands and agrees with answers arrived at by the group)

Encourager (urges silent members to share their thoughts)

When everyone has a specific responsibility, knows what it is, and contributes to a small group, much is accomplished and much is learned.

Summary Partners—One student reads a paragraph, then the partner summarizes the paragraph or interprets its meaning. Partners alternate roles with each paragraph.

The paraphrasing technique also works well in discussions. Anyone who wishes to share a thought must first paraphrase what the previous person said. This sharpens listening skills and demonstrates the power of feedback communication.

Jigsaw—Each person in a small group examines a different concept, Scripture, or part of an issue. Then each teaches the others in the group. Thus, all members teach, and all must learn the others' discoveries. This technique is called a jigsaw because individuals are responsible to their group for different pieces of the puzzle.

JIGSAW EXAMPLE

Here's an example of a jigsaw.

Assign four-person teams. Have teammates each number off from one to four. Have all the Ones go to one corner of the room, all the Twos to another corner, and so on.

Tell team members they're responsible for learning information in their numbered corners and then for teaching their team members when they return to their original teams.

Give the following assignments to various groups:

Ones: Read Psalm 22. Discuss and list the prophecies made about Jesus.

Twos: Read Isaiah 52:13–53:12. Discuss and list the prophecies made about Jesus.

Threes: Read Matthew 27:1-32. Discuss and list the things that happened to Jesus.

Fours: Read Matthew 27:33-66. Discuss and list the things that happened to Jesus.

After the corner groups meet and discuss, instruct all learners to return to their original teams and report what they've learned. Then have each team determine which prophecies about Jesus were fulfilled in the passages from Matthew.

Call on various individuals in each team to report one or two prophecies that were fulfilled.

You Can Do It Too!

All this information may sound revolutionary to you, but it's really not. God has been using active and interactive learning to teach his people for generations. Just look at Abraham and Isaac, Jacob and Esau, Moses and the Israelites, Ruth and Boaz. And then there's Jesus, who used active learning all the time!

Group's Core Belief Bible Study Series makes it easy for you to use active and interactive learning with your group. The active and interactive elements are automatically built in! Just follow the outlines, and watch as your kids grow through experience and positive interaction with others.

FOR DEEPER STUDY

For more information on incorporating active and interactive learning into your work with teenagers, check out these resources:

- *Why Nobody Learns Much of Anything at Church: And How to Fix It,* by Thom and Joani Schultz (Group Publishing) and
- *Do It! Active Learning in Youth Ministry,* by Thom and Joani Schultz (Group Publishing).

your evaluation of core belief

Bible Study Series
for junior high/middle school

the truth about SUFFERING

Group Publishing, Inc.
Attention: Core Belief Talk-back
P.O. Box 481
Loveland, CO 80539
Fax: (970) 669-1994

Please help us continue to provide innovative and useful resources for ministry. After you've led the studies in this volume, take a moment to fill out this evaluation; then mail or fax it to us at the address above. Thanks!

●●●●●●

1. As a whole, this book has been (circle one)

not very helpful								very helpful	
1	2	3	4	5	6	7	8	9	10

2. The best things about this book:

3. How this book could be improved:

4. What I will change because of this book:

5. Would you be interested in field-testing future Core Belief Bible Studies and giving us your feedback? If so, please complete the information below:

Name ______________________________

Street address ______________________________

City ____________________ State __________ Zip __________

Daytime telephone (____) ____________________ Date __________

THANKS!

2

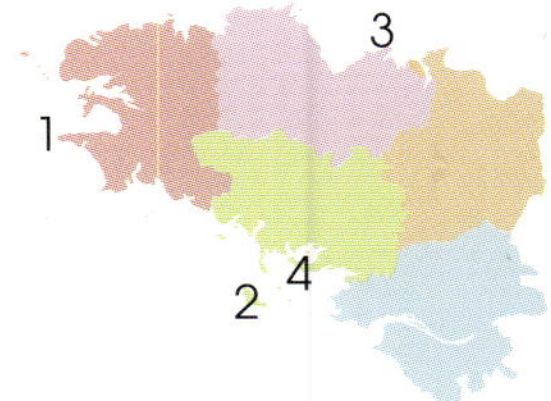

Ci-contre, à gauche : le phare du cap Fréhel dans les Côtes-d'Armor.
En page de titre : entrée du golfe du Morbihan donnant sur l'océan Atlantique, Morbihan.
En couverture : port de plaisance du Crouesty dans la presqu'île de Rhuys, Morbihan. Boucle de l'Aulne près de Châteaulin, Finistère. Château de la Hunaudaye dans les Côtes-d'Armor. Pointe du Raz, Finistère.
En dos de couverture : tour Solidor à Saint-Servan, Côtes d'Armor. Alignements de Kermario à Carnac, Morbihan. Pointe du Van, Finistère.
En premières gardes : à gauche, la pointe du Raz. à droite, le port du Palais et sa citadelle, à Belle-Île, Morbihan.
En dernières gardes : à gauche, la presqu'île de Quiberon dans le Morbihan, à droite, le Mont Saint-Michel . Bien que Normand, à quelques mètres de l'Ille-et-Vilaine, c'est par lui que commence ou s'achève souvent une visite de la Bretagne.

Les chiffres sur les photos renvoient aux cartes représentant les cinq départements bretons. Cela vous permet de positionner en gros les sites. Si le même numéro revient plusieurs fois sur la même page, c'est qu'il s'agit de deux prises de vue du même site ou de sites très voisins.

Imprimé et façonné par Pollina, 85400 Luçon - n° L42968
Imprimé en France.

Julia,
Merry Christmas
2007
Love Paula

Photographies de Maurice Gautier
Texte de Sébastien Recouvrance

Vue du ciel : la Bretagne

Éditions Jean-Paul Gisserot

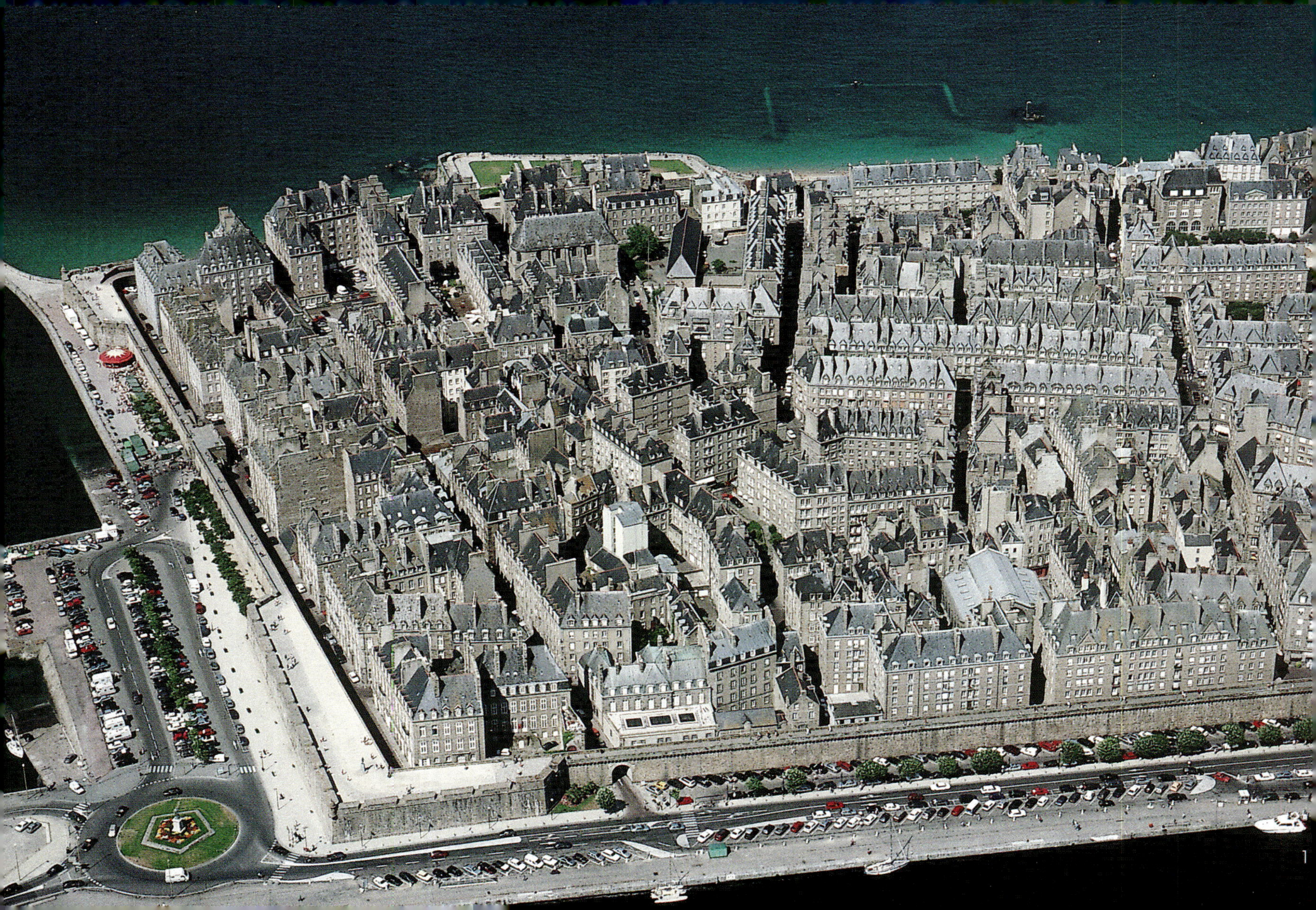

1

Nos remerciements vont tout particulièrement à un pilote émérite, grand connaisseur des campagnes et des littoraux bretons : Philippe Guigon.

C'est un survol en avion de la Bretagne que vous propose ce livre. Les monuments et les paysages s'y montrent sous un aspect inhabituel, et, pour les premiers, tout à fait étranger aux préoccupations esthétiques de leurs architectes. Et pourtant! Il suffit de regarder avec attention la photo de Saint-Malo *intra-muros* ci-contre pour comprendre combien les oiseaux sont avantagés par rapport aux humains pour saisir la logique de l'urbanisme, les impératifs de défense ou le goût de l'apparence.

Il est difficile d'établir un ordre dans un tel programme. Nous avons choisi, de façon tout à fait arbitraire, d'explorer chaque département l'un après l'autre en nous déplaçant dans le sens contraire des aiguilles d'une montre. Ille-et-Vilaine, Côtes d'Armor, Finistère, Morbihan et Loire-Atlantique se succèderont donc. Nous en reconnaissons le côté artificiel, car depuis le ciel on voit très loin, et, bien souvent, plusieurs départements à la fois.

En page de gauche : Saint-Malo *intra-muros*. C'est pour se défendre des invasions normandes que des hommes édifièrent sur un rocher au péril de la mer une cité, plus tard devenue imprenable par la construction de solides remparts. Du Saint-Malo d'origine il ne reste rien. Au cours des siècles. les pauvres maisons de pêcheurs avaient peu à peu été remplacées par de somptueuses demeures, surtout au XVIIIe siècle, attestant de la fortune amassée par les corsaires malouins. Puis la deuxième guerre mondiale est dramatiquement passée par là. En 1945, Saint-Malo était un champ de ruines. Une reconstruction exemplaire a redonné son originale beauté à Saint-Malo.

1

1

Saint-Malo : il s'agit d'un port actif ; derrière la vieille ville, les bassins Vauban et Duguay-Trouin reçoivent cargos, paquebots et yachts de toutes tailles en provenance du monde entier. Au premier plan, au centre, la plage de Bon-Secours est aujourd'hui livrée aux baigneurs qui ignorent les combats sauvages qui s'y sont livrés.

La tour Solidor à Saint-Servan.

Avant les incursions normandes, c'est en ces lieux plus accueillants, appelés alors Aleth, que vivait la population qui devint malouine. Bien qu'ancienne, 1382, la tour Solidor ne date pas de temps aussi reculés. Elle ne plaisait guère aux Malouins, sujets rebelles et indépendants par nature. Cette citadelle a été construite par le duc de Bretagne Jean IV pour contrôler la cité. Sa garnison maîtrisait aussi bien les routes terrestres que maritimes. Aujourd'hui, c'est un paisible musée des Cap-Horniers rassemblant de nombreux souvenirs de ces intrépides voiliers qui bravaient, jusqu'au début du vingtième siècle, les redoutables tempêtes nées de la confrontation des océans Atlantique et Pacifique, pour aller de l'Europe en Californie ou aux îles du Sud. Une très belle chanson de marins évoque leurs aventures : «Nous irons à Valparaiso».

1

Entre Saint-Malo et Dinard, le barrage de la Rance.

Ce monumental moulin à mer emprisonnant les eaux de l'estuaire de la Rance, petit fleuve côtier réduit à un filet d'eau s'il n'y avait là des marées d'amplitudes parmi les plus fortes du monde, est la plus importante usine marémotrice en service. Les kilowatts-heure fournis ne sont pas les meilleurs marchés, mais il s'agit d'énergie renouvelable et le barrage sert également de pont routier. L'apport énergétique représente à peu près 3% de la consommation bretonne, mais, hélas, l'envasement progressif de l'estuaire dû à cette installation n'est guère prometteur d'avenir. En l'occurrence, le renouvelable serait peut-être moins renouvelable qu'on ne le croyait.

Anse de Rochebonne entre Rothéneuf et Saint-Malo. A droite, les bassins du port.

La Côte d'Émeraude a été pionnière du développement touristique. Un peu plus éloignée de Paris que Deauville ou la Côte d'Opale, mais plus belle, elle a retenu l'intérêt des vacanciers dès que les moyens de transports l'ont rendue facilement accessible. Cette photo montre bien l'urbanisation progressive du pays malouin autour de la cité corsaire. C'est une destination favorite des Anglais qui y viennent par un *ferry* régulier, mais aussi des gens du Nord, des Belges, Hollandais et Parisiens.

1

A gauche : le promontoire d'Alet ou d'Aleth en Saint-Servan et la tour Solidor dans la baie de Saint-Malo.

A droite, en haut : le Mont Dol surmonté de son moulin à vent. Il s'agit d'un des trois énormes blocs de roche dure, avec le Mont Saint-Michel et Tombelaine, qui ont résisté à l'érosion entre Cancale et Avranches.

A droite en bas : le menhir de Champ-Dolent près de Dol-de-Bretagne. Haut de 9,5 mètres, il est un des plus grands de Bretagne. En granit, sa masse colossale a été transportée sur plus de 4 km par les hommes du néolithique, sans doute sur des rondins, après avoir été taillée au percuteur sur le lieu d'extraction.

1

2

A gauche : Cancale, centre ostréicole (fournissant, jadis, la table du roi) et charmante station touristique, à l'Ouest de la baie du Mont Saint-Michel.

Ci-dessus : la très belle pointe du Grouin, au Nord de Cancale, ferme la baie du Mont Saint-Michel, côté Bretagne.

Un fleuve : la Vilaine, une écluse, un moulin, un bief. Cette photo du moulin de la Molière en Saint-Senoux près de Pléchatel mériterait de figurer dans un manuel de géographie pour faire comprendre le fonctionnement d'une telle installation. Avant la généralisation de l'électricité, l'eau des fleuves et rivières fournissait l'énergie nécessaire à moudre le grain en farine, et, en un temps où le pain était une des bases de l'alimentation, les meuniers étaient riches.

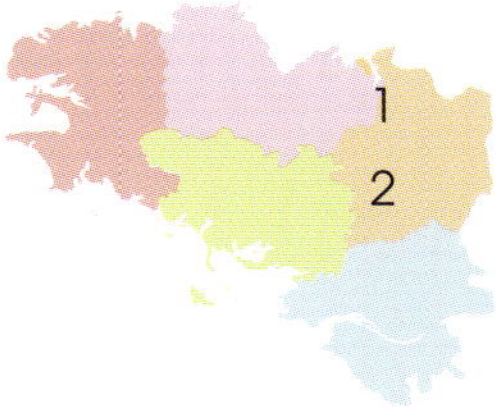

Bécherel sur sa colline de 178 mètres n'est plus ceinte de ses beaux remparts qui ont fait place à une route circulaire.

Dans le Nord de l'Ille-et-Vilaine, cette petite cité s'est spécialisée dans la librairie. La tour de l'église est du XVIe siècle, mais le reste du bâtiment est de 1870.

Autrefois Bécherel travaillait le lin et le chanvre et en tirait d'assez beaux profits qui permirent la construction de belles maisons encore visibles aujourd'hui.

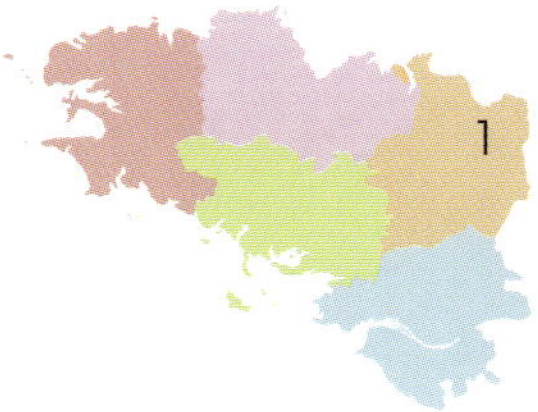

Ces deux vues du château de Combourg montrent les hautes tours de la forteresse où François-René de Chateaubriand passa son enfance. Il y avait sa chambre au sommet de la tour du Chat et dans les «Mémoire d'Outre-Tombe» il évoque le calme morne et lugubre des jours vécus là, en compagnie d'un père taciturne.

La Bourbansais en Pleugueneuc, Montmuran (où Bertrand Duguesclin fut adoubé chevalier en 1357 après sa valeureuse conduite au siège de Rennes) aux Iffs, les alignements du Moulin à Saint-Just, autant de raisons de visiter la campagne d'Ille-et-Vilaine qui recèle toutes ces beautés. Les menhirs, restaurés par Charles-Tanguy Le Roux, datent d'il y a 5 500 ans environ; les châteaux ont vu leur construction s'étaler sur plusieurs siècles, du XVIe au XVIIIe pour La Bourbansais, du XIIe au XVIIIe pour Montmuran.

A la lisière de la forêt de Montauban de Bretagne, à 30 km au Nord-Ouest de Rennes, se cache le château de Montauban dont les deux tours encadrant l'entrée sont de la première moitié du XVᵉ siècle.

Nous ne sommes pas loin de Broons, berceau de Duguesclin, sire de la Motte-Broons, qui devint connétable de France en 1370 de par la volonté de Charles V. Celui-ci lui confia la tâche de reconquérir le territoire français aux mains des Anglais.

Cette photo montre les ruines du château fort du Fretay, à Pancé, près de Bain-de-Bretagne. Il a été construit au XIVᵉ siècle par les seigneurs du lieu et se trouve aujourd'hui, envahi par la végétation, au milieu d'une exploitation agricole.

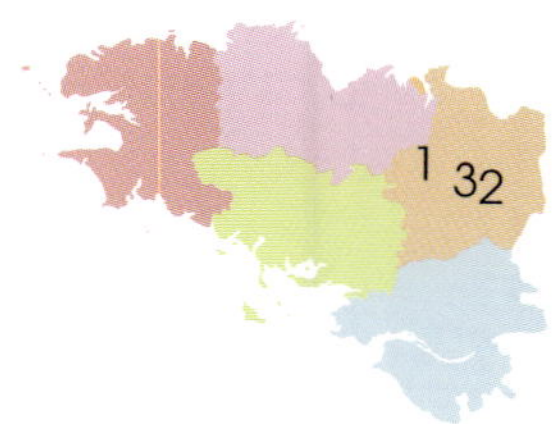

Le château du Boschet à Bourg-des-Comptes est du XVIIe siècle. Construit en 1670, soit une bonne dizaine d'années avant que Louis XIV ne s'installe à Versailles, son style classique s'inspire plutôt des derniers châteaux de la Loire.

Le nom de la commune qui appartenait à la vicomté du Boschet est une francisation abusive de Coms. Sur son territoire la Vilaine fait une boucle tout à fait remarquable, bien connue de tous les pilotes amateurs de la région, à 20 km au Sud de Rennes.

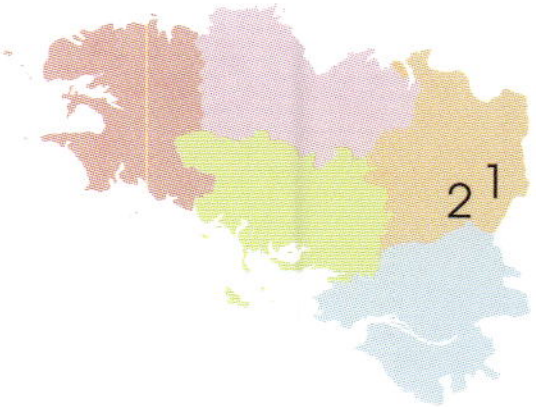

Allée couverte de type Loire, la Roche-aux-Fées à Essé est la plus remarquable de Bretagne. Elle a près de 20 mètres de long, haute de 4 mètres, elle est large de 6, «orientée de telle façon qu'au solstice d'hiver les rayons du soleil viennent illuminer le fond de la chambre pour y réchauffer les défunts déposés autrefois».

(Jacques Briard).

La Bretagne médiévale était indépendante, puisque son rattachement à la France ne date que de 1532, elle avait donc une frontière à défendre face à son grand voisin de l'Est.

Les «marches» de Bretagne sont ainsi semées d'un réseau de citadelles qui ont noms Fougères, Vitré, Châteaubriant, Clisson... Ici, Châteaugiron, au Sud-Est de Rennes, avec ses puissantes tours qui, aujourd'hui, abritent une pacifique coopérative laitière.

La forteresse de Vitré est pour l'essentiel des XIIIe et XVe siècles. C'est un beau témoignage de l'art militaire médiéval, encore en excellent état. Aujourd'hui encerclée dans une ville pleine de charme, elle mériterait d'être davantage connue.

Autre élément du réseau de citadelles des «marches» de Bretagne : Fougères. L'ensemble est extraordinaire. Raoul II y vit son donjon rasé par le roi d'Angleterre Henri Plantagenet en 1166, soit juste un siècle après la victoire de Guillaume le Conquérant à Hasting. Raoul II entreprit la reconstruction de son château et les travaux se poursuivirent jusqu'au XVe siècle. Les Lusignan, la maison d'Alençon, Jean V de Bretagne, les rois de France, le duc de Penthièvre possédèrent tour à tour cette grande baronnie bretonne.

A droite, la Motte Salomon, au village du Gué en Plélan-le-Grand. Ultime trace d'un château féodal gardien des énigmatiques héros, chevaliers de la Table Ronde, Perceval ou Galaad, en quête du Graal dans la mythique forêt de Brocéliande.

Constellée de baigneurs, la plage de Dinard est merveilleusement anachronique avec ses cabines de toile rayée blanche et bleu, pour se changer, en un temps où la pudibonderie du XIXe siècle est quelque peu oubliée. On se croirait revenu au temps de la reine Victoria.

La pêcherie médiévale de l'anse de Vigneux, sur la Rance à Saint-Suliac, montre l'habileté de nos ancêtres à créer des frayères pour favoriser la reproduction des poissons en multipliant les canaux entrelacés. La digue aux formes géométriques servait ensuite à piéger cette manne envoyée par Dieu.

Rennes.

La capitale de la Bretagne est une cité moderne et active dont l'urbanisme ne fait pas penser à une petite cité campagnarde. Les tours, les barres et les centres commerciaux ont envahi l'espace, ici comme ailleurs. La mer est loin, les étés sont chauds et les étudiants sont nombreux. Quelle est leur soif d'apprendre dans ces grandes cités universitaires ? Ou s'agit-il davantage d'un désir de survivre! Mais ne soyons pas nostalgiques devant l'inéluctable. C'est la contrepartie du confort. Lætititia Bonaparte, la mère de Napoléon 1er, dont chacun sait qu'il était né en Bretagne à Sainte-Sève, près de Morlaix, aurait dit avec son accent corse «*pourvou que ça doure*».

L'abbaye Saint-Sauveur de Redon a été fondée par saint Conwoïon dans la première moitié du IXe siècle. Nominoë, roi de Bretagne la prit sous sa protection par un acte de reconnaissance du 18 juin 832. Détruite par les Normands, l'abbaye fut reconstruite à la période romane. Du XIIe siécle, il ne reste que la nef et la très belle tour lanterne, carrée, aux angles arrondis, ce qui est exceptionnel et en fait un des plus beaux édifices romans de Bretagne. L'abbaye abrite, depuis 1804, un lycée.

L'église Saint-Pierre de Langon est pour partie romane. Son originale tour de la croisée du transept, carrée aux angles vifs, possède douze clochetons qui permettent de l'identifier facilement d'avion. Non loin, la chapelle Sainte-Agathe date de l'époque gallo-romaine et serait un avatar de thermes privés avec une fresque consacréà à Vénus, encore visible, ce qui expliquerait son ancien nom de Saint-Vener.

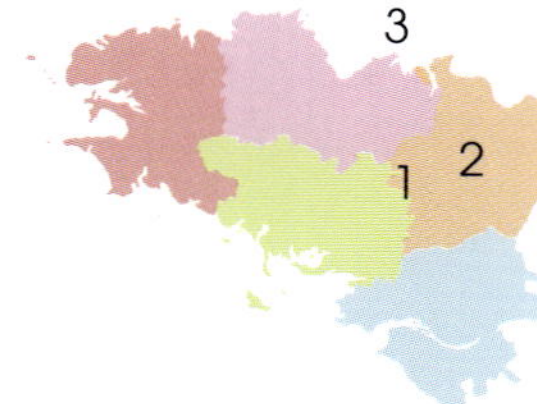

Les deux photos de gauche ont été prises en survolant Brocéliande, à Paimpont.

En haut, les forges, déjà mentionnées dans des documents du XVIe siècle, exploitaient le minerai de fer local, la forêt fournissant le combustible pour l'élaboration du métal. La prospérité des forges de Paimpont fut grande, à l'époque classique, quand elles fournirent l'arsenal de Brest pour la construction de la flotte royale.

En bas, l'imposante église abbatiale de Paimpont date du XIIIe siècle.

A droite :

Cette vue du bocage du bassin de Rennes au printemps montre la diversité des cultures à laquelle la Bretagne reste attachée. Le jaune du colza y donne une note de gaité.

Nous arrivons dans les Côtes-d'Armor.

Formidable sur son éperon rocheux s'avançant au milieu des flots, le Fort-La-Latte, à l'Est du cap Fréhel, a été construit aux XIIIe et XIVe siècles par la famille des Goyon-Matignon, ceux-là mêmes qui ont légué leur nom à l'hôtel du Premier ministre français.

2

3

Dinan, sous-préfecture des Côtes-d'Armor, est une ville magnifique par son site, ses remparts, ses maisons médiévales, son château de la duchesse Anne et son quartier du Jerzual qui descend vers le port. Dominant la vallée de la Rance, le jardin Anglais, derrière la basilique romane Saint-Sauveur, offre un panorama exceptionnel. Bertrand Duguesclin était dinanais de cœur et c'est place des Lices qu'il livra, en vainqueur, son premier tournoi à quinze ans. Auguste Pavie, explorateur de l'Asie est né à Dinan, comme Michel Renouard, auteur du plus important guide de Bretagne dû à la plume d'un seul écrivain. Le beffroi, de la fin du XVe siècle, mérite une attention toute particulière.

Le viaduc élevé enjambant la Rance à l'Est de Dinan conduit à Rennes ou au Mont Saint-Michel. Un flot de touristes devrait donc l'emprunter pour assurer à la ville, une des plus belles de France, une économie prospère, mais les difficultés de circulation et surtout de stationnement freinent ce développement.

Vue aérienne du sanctuaire gallo-romain du Haut-Bécherel à Corseul. La tour polygonale, une *cella*, dite Temple de Mars, était connue depuis longtemps, mais la vue aérienne a révélé d'importantes dépendances. La région semble avoir été très peuplée dès le premier siècle avant notre ère.

Jules César parle des Coriosolites dans la «Guerre des Gaules». Cette tribu gauloise colonisait Jersey, avait sa monnaie, vendait ses produits jusqu'en Angleterre.

Devenue cité romaine, Corseul connut la *pax romana* pendant un demi millénaire avant d'être emportée dans la tourmente barbare.

Plus impressionnant qu'un monstre antédiluvien, le cap Fréhel, masse rocheuse pelée de porphyre et ce grès rouge domine la Manche de ses 70 mètres. Il faut aller jusqu'aux endroits les plus sauvages de la presqu'île de Crozon, en Finistère, pour trouver des sites plus terribles.

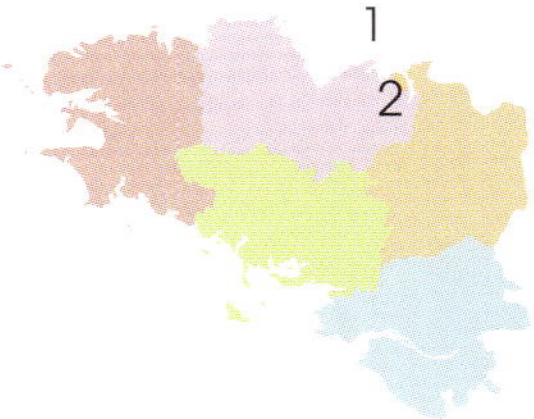

Redoutable forteresse défendant le Penthièvre, le château de La Hunaudaye, construit par Pierre de Tournemine, chef d'œuvre de l'architecture militaire de la fin du moyen âge, a subi les avanies du temps. Pour éviter qu'il ne serve aux chouans, les révolutionnaires firent sauter un pan de sa courtine en 1793, puis, ouvert à tous les vents, il fut pillé par les paysans voisins. Il servit de carrière jusqu'au début du XXe siècle avant de devenir propriété de l'État.

Guingamp, dont l'origine du nom est très difficile à connaître (camp béni pour certains, camp blanc pour d'autres), était un camp retranché destiné à protéger les populations du Sud Goëlo des invasions vikings. Ville ducale prospère à la fin du moyen âge, sa basilique Notre-Dame de Bon-Secours date des XIVe et XVe siècles.

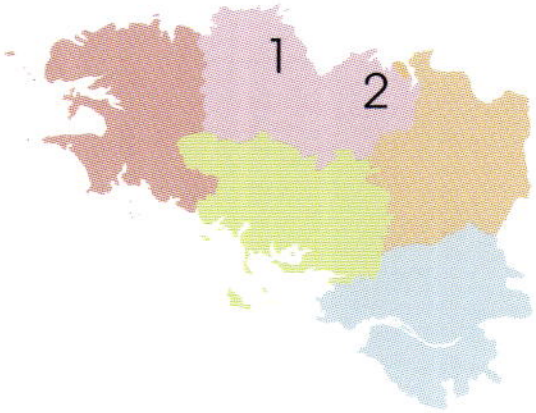

Château de Bien-Assis à Erquy.

Gilles Visdelou, seigneur d'un château en ces lieux, servait le roi de France et combattit le terrible duc de Mercœur, chef de la Ligue en Bretagne. Son domaine en partie détruit par ses adversaires, Visdelou (parfois orthographié Viselou) le fit reconstruire à partir de 1620 en grès rose de la région. L'ensemble actuel a grande allure, le mariage des styles y étant harmonieux.

Le château du Guildo près de Saint-Cast est une forteresse du XVe siècle qui fut rasée au XVIIe sur ordre de Richelieu. Ce fut la résidence du jeune prince Gilles de Bretagne, né en 1425, fils de Jean V, frère du duc François 1er. Gilles avait été élevé en Angleterre et aimait la vie. Il vivait au milieu de nombreux amis d'Outre-Manche et le duc, le considérant comme du parti des Anglais, le fit étouffer entre deux matelas le 25 avril 1450. Belle fraternité!

1

2

La base de loisirs de Beau Rivage sur le lac de Guerlédan.

Ce lac artificiel a été créé en 1923 pour alimenter un barrage hydroélectrique et constituer une importante réserve d'eau douce en Bretagne de l'intérieur.

Le bocage de la haute vallée de l'Oust où la rivière paresse entre les prairies.

Ligne d'éoliennes sur les hauteurs de Saint-Gelven, au Nord du lac de Guerlédan

Le lac de Guerlédan matérialise la frontière entre les Côtes-d'Armor et le Morbihan. Il recouvre les anciennes gorges du Blavet sur 13 km et une superficie de 400 hectares. Sa création a coupé le canal de Nantes à Brest, construit sous le premier Empire, en supprimant 18 écluses.

1

L'abbaye de Bon-Repos, fondée en 1172 par Alain de Rohan, a connu bien des vicissitudes. Un frère de Mazarin en fût abbé. Les bâtiments du XVIIIe ont connu la ruine, mais une association entreprend courageusement de les restaurer.

L'abbaye de Boquen, fondée en 1137, recueillit la dépouille de Gilles de Bretagne assassiné sur ordre de son frère en 1450. Bien national à la Révolution, elle servit de carrière avant d'être sauvée par un retour des moines en 1936, puis l'arrivée des sœurs de Bethléem.

2

3

Le canal de Nantes à Brest vers Glomel. Les États de Bretagne rêvaient de cette voie d'eau navigable depuis longtemps lorsqu'elle fut enfin réalisée sous l'Empire. Il fallait épargner aux marchandises les périls de la mer : tempêtes et flottes ennemies, à une époque où les routes étaient de mauvais sentiers, impraticables pour les charges lourdes.

Tréguier, sa cathédrale et son clocher, sur les rives du Jaudy. La ville, ancien évêché, a été fondée par saint Tugdual au VIe siècle. Un ancien chanoine du chapître, Siéyès, devenu membre de l'Assemblée nationale, prépara la Déclaration des droits de l'homme. C'est le pays de saint Yves, patron des avocats, et d'Ernest Renan. Le beau clocher de la cathédrale a été construit avec les revenus d'un impôt sur les cartes à jouer, ce qui explique que ses bâtisseurs l'ont ajouré de trèfles, piques, cœurs et carreaux. Le cloître de Tréguier est un des plus beaux de France.

Le château de Caradeuc, en Plouasne, est à cheval sur l'Ille-et-Vilaine et les Côtes-d'Armor. Construit en 1723 pour Louis Caradeuc de la Chalotais, c'est le Versailles breton avec un parc royal.

L'abbaye de Beauport, près de Paimpol, a été fondée par Alain de Penthièvre au tout début du XIIIe siècle. Les moines prémontrés l'ont animée jusqu'à la Révolution, puis elle servit de poudrière.

Rachetée en 1845 par le comte Poninski, elle est aujourd'hui propriété du Conservatoire du littoral qui l'entretient avec soins.

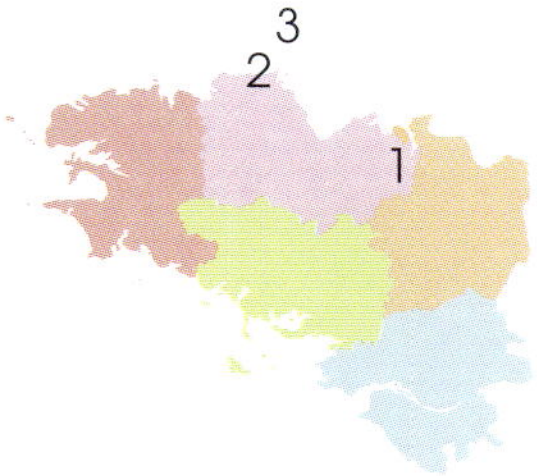

Saint-Budoc dut se croire au paradis lorsqu'il fonda au VIe siècle une école monastique sur cet îlot de Lavret dans l'archipel de Bréhat.

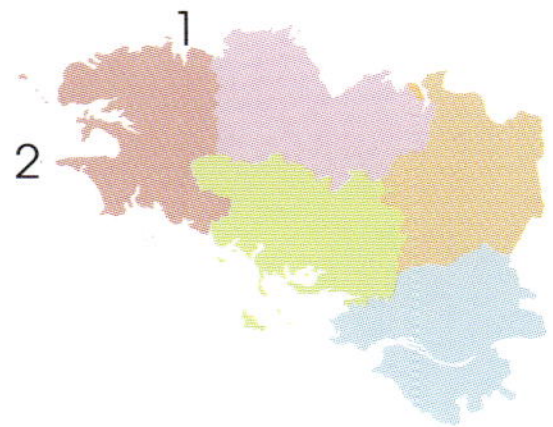

C'est par le Nord que nous abordons le Finistère.

Le cairn mégalithique de Barnenez en Plouezoc'h, au Nord de Morlaix, est extraordinaire. Construit 2000 ans avant les pyramides à degrés d'Égypte, ce tumulus en est l'ébauche déja bien élaborée. Long de 90 mètres, large de 40 et haut de 7, il comporte onze chambres funéraires en tholos et sa masse est aux alentours de 50 000 tonnes.

Ce monument avait été oublié des archéologues. En 1950, considéré comme un tas de cailloux providentiel par un entrepreneur, il servit de carrière. Ceci explique la double échancrure circulaire qui l'ampute en haut à droite sur la photo. Heureusement le massacre fut stoppé, et une restauration exemplaire rendit sa dignité au monument, témoignage irremplaçable de la civilisation du néolithique dans nos régions.

À droite, nous allons plus au Sud, à la Pointe du Raz. C'est le plus méridional des trois caps que le Finistère avance dans l'Atlantique. Ce formidable éperon rocheux est connu de tous les marins du monde qui redoutent les eaux terribles du *Raz de Sein*, passage mortellement dangereux entre la pointe et l'île de Sein.

2

Trois sanctuaires bretons : l'abbaye de Landévennec, fondée par saint Guénolé, fils de saint Fragan et de sainte Gwen, au Ve siècle; la chapelle du Mont Saint-Michel-de-Brasparts; l'abbaye Saint-Tanguy à la pointe Saint-Mathieu, surmontée de son phare.

La chapelle du Mont Saint-Michel-de-Brasparts est toute simple, mais vous y aurez une vue sur tout le Finistère, ou presque. Landévennec est un des plus hauts lieux spirituels de bretagne, quant à la pointe Saint-Matthieu, c'est un paysage marin sublime.

Les Tas de Pois se trouvent au bout de la pointe de Pen-Hir dans la presqu'île de Crozon. Ce sont d'énormes blocs rocheux qui avancent *decrescendo* dans les flots de l'océan.

À droite, cette boucle de l'Aulne, près de Châteaulin, est encore sensible aux mouvements des marées qui font monter et descendre le niveau de l'eau deux fois par jour.

La magnifique place de Locronan où trônent l'église et la chapelle du Pénity. Tous les édifices sont en granit, témoignant des splendeurs de la ville aux XVIe, XVIIe et XVIIIe siècles, quand ses tisserands fournissaient en voiles de lin les navires de commerce ou royaux.

Saint-Pol-de-Léon, dans le Nord Finistère est une des sept étapes du *tro breiz*, (tour de Bretagne), pèlerinage consacré aux sept saints fondateurs de la Bretagne; ici saint Pol Aurélien, moine gallois venu évangéliser la région au VIe siècle. Nous distinguons bien sur la photo les deux principaux monuments religieux de la ville : au premier plan le *kreizkêr* avec son superbe clocher d'inspiration normande qui culmine à 78 mètres de hauteur et, plus éloignée, la cathédrale.

Deux côtes rocheuses au Nord de la presqu'île d'Audierne. La pointe du Van proche de la pointe du Raz et de la baie des Trépassés. Le Cap Sizun, légèrement plus à l'Est, à l'entrée de la baie de Douarnenez, offre ses falaises escarpées à une réserve d'oiseaux de mer.

Castel Meur, le Grand Château en breton, à Cléden-Cap-Sizun, est un mince éperon rocheux qui, facile à défendre, servit de refuge aux hommes préhistoriques. Les traces des fossés qu'ils ont creusés il y a quelques milliers d'années se voient encore, tout comme les fonds de cabane d'époque médiévale.

La chapelle Saint-They, à la pointe du Van, se dresse sur une imposante falaise qui domine une mer en permanence démontée. Les vents, les courants et les houles s'y affrontent depuis des millions d'années grignotant le granit avec une patience de rat.

Bénodet. Ici, l'Odet se jette dans l'Atlantique. (*Penodet*, en breton, signifie la «tête de l'Odet»). Le climat y est d'une grande douceur. À gauche, Sainte-Marine, mauvaise traduction de Saint-Moran, où Émile Zola séjourna au château de Kerbirinic.

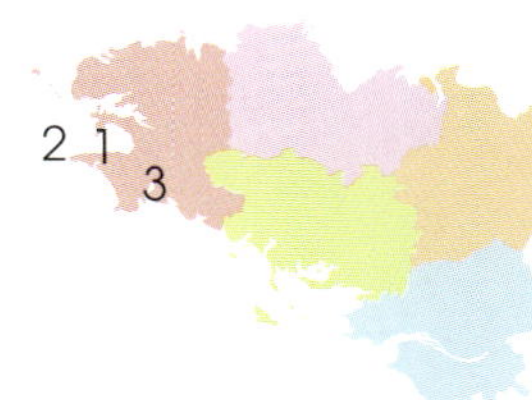

1

2

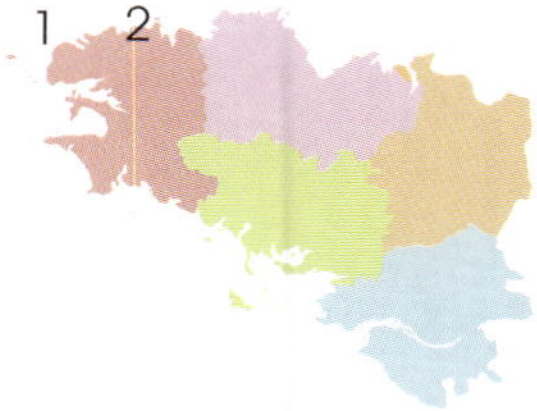

Île Gaignog ou Guennoc, au large de Landéda dans le Pays des Abers. Une nouvelle fois, les quatre tumulus vieux de 6000 ans, au sommet de cet îlot, témoignent du goût des hommes préhistoriques de se faire enterrer dans des sites remarquables, isolés, avec une vue superbe, pour affronter l'éternité. Comme à Barnenez, qui n'est guère éloigné, les dolmens à couloirs, une douzaine, s'achèvent par des chambres en tholos, ici étêtées. Comment ne pas rêver à l'étrange vie de nos ancêtres, au final très proches de nous dans la longue histoire du monde!

La douceur du climat de la région de Saint-Pol-de-Léon y a autorisé le développement d'une agriculture maraîchère florissante. Sous l'influence d'un courant marin chaud venant des Caraïbes, le «courant du golfe», artichauts et choux-fleurs poussent ici comme le blé en Beauce ou la vigne en Bourgogne. Tout commença par l'oignon, qui, se conservant bien, servait de vivres frais à bord des bateaux, puis le choux-fleurs vint d'Italie du Sud et l'artichaut de Sicile ou des Canaries. Cela sert d'avoir eu des marins curieux des plantes du bout du monde.

Vue d'ensemble de la pointe du Van.
Un mot s'impose : terrible!

1

Quel contraste entre le lugubre phare de la Vieille au large de la pointe du Raz, témoin de tous les naufrages dans le Raz de Sein, séjour sévère pour ses gardiens au milieu des tourbillons infernaux aux écumes nourries de cadavres de marins, et le port de Concarneau!

Aujourd'hui port de pêche et de plaisance, Concarneau dont la ville close fut une repaire de brigands est devenue une étape obligée du tourisme en Bretagne. Restaurants et galeries d'art ont pris la place des aventuriers des mers.

2

3

La plage de Pentrez, au fond de la baie de Douarnenez, est bordée par les eaux qui recouvrirent la ville d'Ys au temps du roi Gradlon.

L'estuaire du Goyen à Audierne est le premier hâvre sérieux pour les bateaux au sortir du Raz de Sein.

Douarnenez, grand port de pêche sur la baie qui porte son nom est une ville très active. Son nom viendrait peut-être de *douar nevez*, la terre nouvelle, pour avoir servi de refuge aux habitants d'Ys une fois leur cité engloutie. Nous sommes au pays de Dahut, de saint Guénolé et de Gradlon...

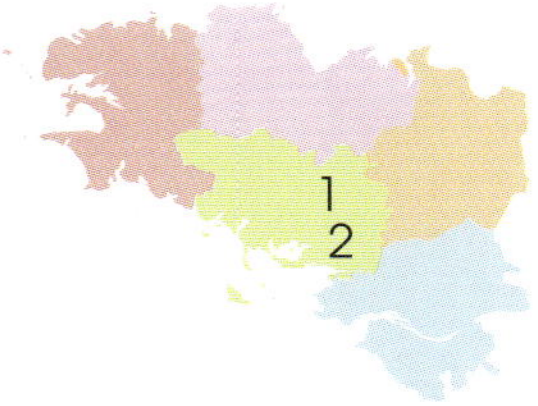

Le Morbihan, où nous arrivons, tient son nom du golfe éponyme, en breton : petite mer.

La forteresse de Josselin doit son nom au prénom du fils de son créateur, Guéthenoc, vicomte de Porhoët. Mais de la citadelle de l'an mil, il ne reste rien, Henri II d'Angleterre étant passé par là. C'est au XIVe siècle qu'Olivier de Clisson en fit un château fort de première importance. En 1629, Richelieu ordonna la destruction du donjon et d'une partie des fortifications. C'est aujourd'hui le fief des Rohan.

Rochefort-en-Terre, site médiéval important n'en conserve que peu de souvenirs. Le château, reconstruit au XVIIe a été victime du feu avant d'être restauré au XXe. Le site, à l'Ouest de Redon, est admirable.

Après les moissons dans les riches campagnes du Porhoët, la terre garde les couleurs dorées des chaumes. Une éolienne donne sa note de modernité à un paysage très rural. De son nom qui signifie «pays d'outre forêt», le Porhoët ne porte guère témoignage puisque les anciennes forêts ont cédé la place aux bocages puis aux vastes parcelles remembrées des années 1970.

Ploërmel, ville dont la tradition rapporte qu'elle fut fondée au VIe siècle par saint Armel (*Plou-Armel* signifiant la paroisse, ou le peuple, d'Armel), entoure l'église Saint-Armel de styles gothique flamboyant et renaissance. Ce fut la ville des frères Lamennais, au XIXe siècle.

Parcs à huîtres dans le golfe du Morbihan. Leur production est d'excellente qualité.

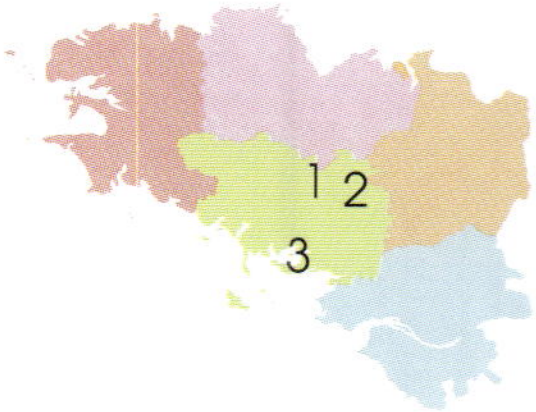

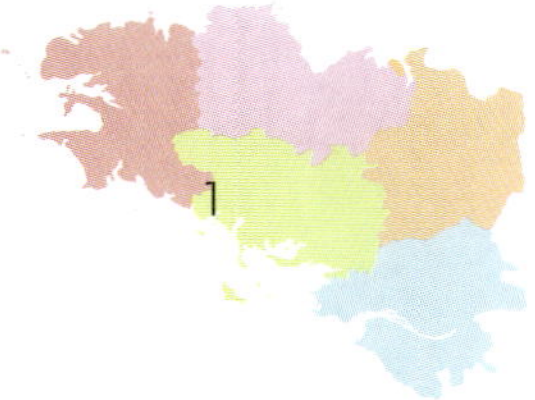

Louis XIV ordonna la création de Lorient en 1666. Il s'agissait d'enrichir la France d'un grand port maritime sur le vaste estuaire formé par l'embouchure du Scorff et du Blavet. Son nom vient de l'Orient, destination quasi exclusive des vaisseaux de la Compagnie des Indes qui s'y fixa très vite. Port de pêche très important, chantier de construction navale essentiel pour notre défense, Lorient prospéra, et son arsenal livra parmi les plus belles unités de notre marine.

La deuxième guerre mondiale fut terrible pour la ville. Pendant l'occupation, les allemands y édifièrent une base sous-marine géante, à Kéroman (photo du bas), pour abriter leurs redoutables submersibles entre deux missions de torpillage des flottes alliées.

À la Libération, il y eut là d'effroyables combats. Le «poche de Lorient» résista longtemps. La ville fut rasée, de nombreux habitants furent tués.

Du passé, il ne reste que quelques beaux hôtels de la Compagnie des Indes. Un festival inter-celtique se déroule chaque année à Lorient.

Cette double page met en évidence le goût des Bretons pour la mer et la plaisance. La Bretagne est entourée de tous côtés, sauf à l'Est, par la mer. Comment son peuple ne serait-il pas marin! Les relations des marins avec la mer sont faites de contradictions, ils ne peuvent s'en passer et ils la craignent, ils la respectent et ils s'en servent. Trop de Bretons ont péri en mer mais la mer leur a permis de découvrir le monde, leur a aussi permis de vivre! Même à l'intérieur des terres on travaillait pour la mer en tissant le lin pour les voiles, en salant le cochon, récoltant les oignons pour les cambuses, en sciant les arbres des forêts pour les charpentiers de marine, en forgeant le fer. Toute l'économie bretonne dépendait de la mer, jusqu'aux transports, aisés par cabotage, infernaux sur de mauvais chemins de terre, boueux, étroits et pleins d'ornières, voire fréquentés par les brigands!

Vus du ciel, selon les dispositifs d'amarrage, les bateaux forment de jolies et variées figures géométriques. Ici, en haut, La Trinité-sur-Mer avec ses grands et sages alignements, en bas, Hœdic, une des îles au large de Quiberon où l'on dirait que les voiliers viennent manger autour de trois bouées.

De gauche à droite :

La Rivière du Vincin et la presqu'île de Conleau abritent les embarcations des Vannetais. C'est à quelques kilomètres de chez eux et ils sont nombreux à confier leurs bateaux à ces eaux calmes qui suivent sans passion le cycle des marées.

Cette vue de La Trinité-sur-Mer montre au premier plan les grands trimarans de régates, en apparence bien fragiles, mais qui n'hésitent pas à affronter les tempêtes des caps Horn ou de Bonne Espérance.

Au Nord-Est de Belle-Île, le port de Sauzon est bien abrité, face à Quiberon, et de nombreux marins lui confient la garde de leurs bâtiments, parfois leur bien le plus cher.

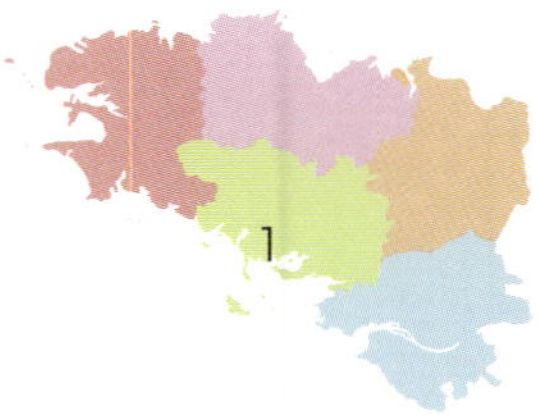

Le Morbihan, c'est aussi le département de Carnac avec ses alignements mégalithiques, les plus grands du monde.

Ici, les alignements de Kermario comportent 1029 pierres et s'étendent sur 1200 mètres de long et 100 mètres de large. En bas, à droite de la photo, on distingue le dolmen de Kermario qui borde la route. Pour donner une échelle et comprendre la taille de ces mégalithes, il faut savoir que ce monument, qui semble bien petit, mesure 8,70 mètres de long! Elle était à l'origine recouverte d'un tumulus protégeant le sommeil des défunts, mais, comme bien souvent, l'érosion a fini par disperser ce rempart bien fragile de la paix éternelle.

Dans le Morbihan, comme ailleurs, les hommes ont souvent voulu domestiquer la mer. Mieux vaut le faire avec prudence et dans des coins où elle se laisse faire!

La photo du haut montre le port de plaisance artificiel du Crouesty qui a été creusé sur la commune d'Arzon à l'extrémité de la presqu'île de Rhuys, côté océan, pour éviter les eaux dangereuses au passage de la barre qui ferme le Golfe. En moins d'un demi siècle les landes sauvages sont devenues surpeuplées.

En bas, ces pêcheries anciennes, révélées par la photo aérienne dans la rivière de Conleau, sont très difficiles à dater. Sont-elles préhistoriques ? Pour partie peut-être. Plus vraisemblablement médiévales, elles servaient à piéger le poisson en évitant d'aller se confronter aux nombreux périls de la mer.

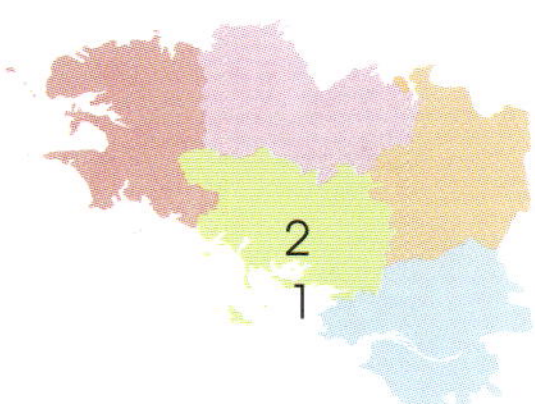

Le site mégalithique de la Table des Marchand, à Locmariaquer, est exceptionnel. Il réunit autour du dolmen le cairn d'Er Grah et le Grand menhir brisé, le plus grand de Bretagne, qui mesurait plus de 20 mètres de haut pour un poids de 350 tonnes!

Vannes, préfecture du Morbihan, étape du Tro Breiz, autour de sa cathédrale dédiée à saint Patern, l'un des sept saints fondateurs de la Bretagne au VIe siècle.

Château de Suscinio dans la presqu'île de Rhuys.

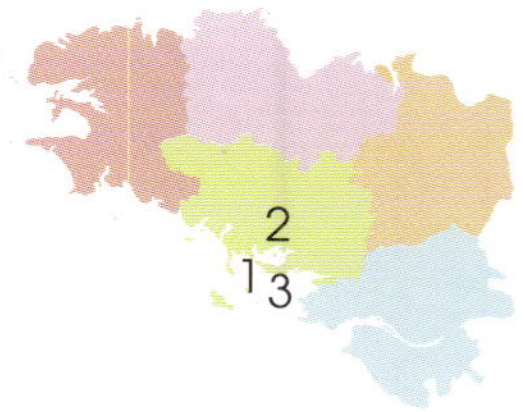

Le château de Suscinio, devenu propriété du département du Morbihan, fait l'objet d'une très belle restauration. Construit par le duc de Bretagne Pierre Mauclerc au début du XIIIe siècle il fut agrandi par ses descendants. Tombé aux mains des Anglais, il fut reconquis pour la couronne de France par Bertrand Duguesclin en 1373. Jean de Montfort le reprit avec l'aide des Anglais et son fils, le futur duc de Bretagne Arthur III, y naquit. Après bien des péripéties, le château devint carrière sous la Révolution, puis, de nos jours, très intéressant musée.

Le massif château des Rohan à Pontivy montre la puissance de cette famille au XVe siècle lorsqu'elle choisit de faire de cette ville sa capitale. Pour des raisons stratégiques, Napoléon 1er s'intéressa à cette sous-préfecture du Morbihan à laquelle il donna son nom en l'appelant Napoléonville. Après quelques éclipses dues aux changements de régimes, ce nom lui resta jusqu'en 1870 où la cité redevint Pontivy, en hommage à saint Yvi, moine gallois qui y construisit le premier pont sur le Blavet.

1

2

Le dolmen restauré du Petit-Mont en Arzon, au bout de la presqu'île de Rhuys, est un autre témoignage de l'importance des populations du néolithique dans la région. Une datation au radio carbone en fait remonter les parties les plus anciennes à 4800 ans environ. Ce tombeau a été remanié à plusieurs reprises. Il a servi pendant plus de mille ans comme c'est le cas de la plupart des cairns préhistoriques. Nous devons son étude et sa restauration à J. Lecornec.

La pointe du Vieux-Château à Belle-Île est un éperon barré de l'Âge du Fer. *Coh Castel* en Breton. Jacques Briard nous apprend qu'elle couvre cinq hectares et qu'elle était fortifiée vers l'intérieur par des talus et des fossés garantissant la sécurité de ses habitants. Talus, par endroits, encore visibles.

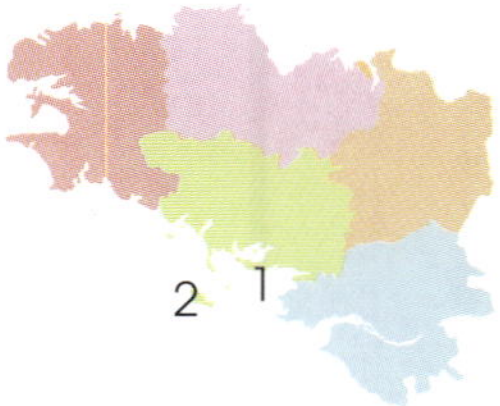

photo : Jean L'Helgouac'h

Vue rapprochée du Grand Menhir Brisé de Locmariaquer.

Les études récentes de Jean L'Helgouac'h et de Charles-Tanguy Le Roux ont bien montré qu'il avait été abattu puis débité en vue d'être réutilisé, vers 4500 av J.C., dans la construction des grands dolmens.

Le château de Comper au bord d'un étang dans la forêt de Paimpont.

Le site a été «récupéré» par la légende arthurienne et ses chevaliers de la Table Ronde. Un premier château aurait été construit ici par Diane la chasseresse.

Viviane plongea dans le lac avec Lancelot pour rejoindre une forteresse bâtie au fond des eaux par l'enchanteur Merlin!.

Les forges des Salles, près de Gouarec, dans la forêt de Quénécan, sont un des plus vieux centres métallurgiques de Bretagne. On y traitait le fer avec le bois de la forêt et le calcaire d'une carrière voisine. Il fallait que les matières premières soient proches à une époque où les transports étaient difficiles.

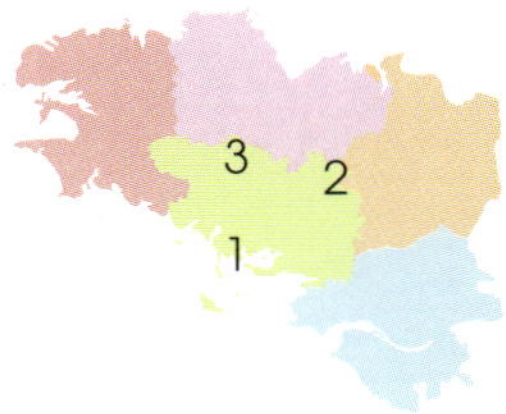

photo : Gilles Leroux

Nous achevons notre vol par la Loire-Atlantique.

photo : Gilles Leroux

Guérande et sa presqu'île. Au Nord de la Loire, dans sa partie Ouest, le département comporte une vaste zône marécageuse, la Grande Brière, puis les marais salants de Guèrande dont la production est aujourd'hui mondialement connue. On exploite ici le sel depuis la préhistoire.

Les remparts circulaires de Guérande sont presqu'intacts. C'est un incomparable exemple de fortifications médiévales des XIVe et XVe siècles.

Au centre, l'église Saint-Aubin dédiée au patron de la ville.

Le château de Clisson date du XIIIe siècle. Cette ancienne demeure d'Olivier de Clisson, est aujourd'hui en ruines, mais elle garde fière allure.

Pendant la Révolution elle fut le théâtre d'horreurs. Son puits servit de charniers pour les royalistes vaincus.

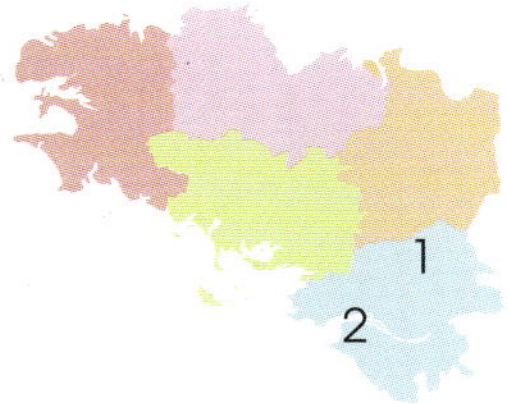

Châteaubriant est une cité du Nord de la Loire-Atlantique. Le château médiéval (XIe et XIIIe siècles) a été agrandi à la Renaissance. Françoise de Foix y habita avant de devenir la maîtresse du roi de France François 1er. Quand celui-ci la délaissa, elle revint finir ses jours à Châteaubriant - qu'elle trouvait bien triste - auprès de son mari légitime, Jean de Laval.

Le pont de Saint-Nazaire franchit la Loire à son embouchure entre Montoir de Bretagne et Saint-Brévin-les-Pins. Construit en 1974, il mesure 3356 mètres avec une travée centrale de 404 mètres et un tirant d'air de 61 mètres, au dessus des plus basses eaux, afin de permettre le passage des bateaux jusqu'au port de Nantes. Ce fut longtemps le plus long pont de France. Exemple à suivre : le péage initial a été supprimé en 1994 et le passage est aujourd'hui gratuit.

photo : Gilles Leroux

photo : Gilles Leroux

La Motte Glain reconstruit dans la mode du temps, à la fin du XVe, par Pierre de Rohan, maréchal de Gié, est à mi chemin entre le château fort - avec tours et poivrières - et la demeure de plaisance. Les murs en schiste et tuffeau, les toits d'ardoise, une architecture harmonieuse en font un site remarquable.

Château de la Groulais à Blain.

Près du canal de Nantes à Brest, cette belle demeure témoigne de la prospérité d'Olivier IV de Clisson, connétable de France, dont la mère armait à la piraterie. Il bâtit le Petit Castel (Logis du Roi et Logis de la Reine) ainsi que quatre tours d'angles et des remparts. La Renaissance modifia profondément l'aspect des lieux. Le château resta ensuite plusieurs siècles propriété des Rohan.

Les chantiers de l'Atlantique, autrefois de Penhoët, à Saint-Nazaire.

Nous finissons ce tour de Bretagne sur une note industrielle un peu nostalgique, très importante pour la région : la construction navale.

Ici, ont été construits le paquebot France et les plus gros pétroliers du monde. Les chantiers sont parmi les plus importants d'Europe. Tout y est colossal, les ateliers comme les formes d'assemblage (la plus grande a 1200 mètres de long).

photo : Gilles Leroux

photo : Gilles Leroux

Aujourd'hui, concurrencée par les pays émergents, la «navale» a du mal à survivre sous le ciel de Bretagne, en dépit d'un savoir-faire reconnu par le monde entier.

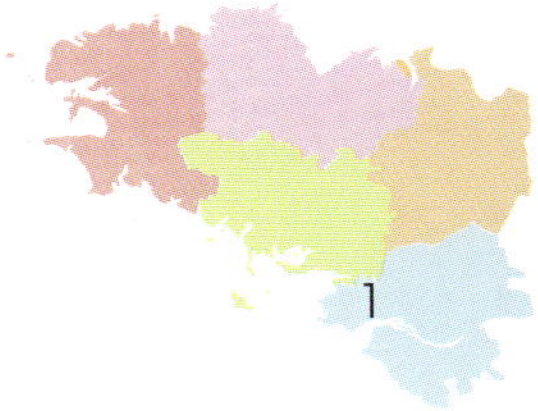

Côte des Légendes
Côte de Granit Rose
Côte d'Émeraude
Côte de Cornouaille
Côte Sauvage
Côte d'Amour
Île de Batz
Roscoff
St-Pol-de-Léon
Plouescat
Plouguerneau
Lesneven
Lannilis
le Folgoët
Ouessant
Molène
Ploudalmezeau
Plabennec
Landivisiau
Lampaul-Guimiliau
la Martyre
St-Thégonnec
Guimiliau
St-Sauveur
Commana
Morlaix
St-Renan
Le Conquet
Brest
Landerneau
Plougastel
Daoulas
Sizun
Pte St-Mathieu
Camaret
Crozon
Landévennec
Pte de Pen-Hir
Argol
Morgat
Châteaulin
Pleyben
Cap de la Chèvre
Douarnenez
Châteauneuf-du-Faou
Aulne
Locronan
Pte du Raz
Sein
Audierne
Pont-Croix
QUIMPER
Pouldreuzic
Pont-l'Abbé
N-D-de-Tronoën
Bénodet
Fouesnant
Concarneau
Penmarch
Le Guilvinec
Glénan
Trégastel
Ploumanach
Perros-Guirec
Pleumeur-Bodou
Tréguier
Lézardrieux
Île de Bréhat
l'Arcouest
Paimpol
Barnenez
Lannion
Locquirec
St-Michel-en-Grève
Lanmeur
Plestin-les-Grèves
la Roche-Derrien
Pontrieux
Plouha
Bégard
Lanvollon
Plouaret
Guingamp
Belle-Isle-en-Terre
Châtelaudren
Bourbriac
Huelgoat
Callac
Bulat-Pestivien
Quintin
Lanrivain
Carhaix-Plouguer
St-Nicolas-du-Pélem
Canal de Nantes à Brest
Rostrenen
Gouarec
Lac de Guerlédan
Mûr-de-Bretagne
Gourin
Scaër
le Faouët
Kernascléden
Rosporden
Quimperlé
Isole
Plouay
Pont-Aven
Le Pouldu
Lorient
Lanester
Hennebont
Port-Louis
Groix
Blavet
Scorff
St-Quay-Portrieux
Etable
ST-BRIEUC
Pléneuf-Val-André
Erquy
Cap Fréhel
St-Cast
Matignon
St-Lunaire
St-Briac
St-Malo
Dinard
Le Guildo
Ploubalay
Plancoët
Lamballe
Dinan
Rance
Jugon
Moncontour
Uzel
Plouguenast
le Gouray
Collinée
Broons
Caulnes
Évran
St-Caradec
Loudéac
Merdrignac
la Chèze
la Trinité-Porhoët
Pontivy
Rohan
Mauron
Paimpont
Josselin
Campénéac
Locminé
Baud
Plumelec
Malestroit
Guer
Ste-d'Anne-d'Auray
Auray
Elven
Etel
Carnac
la Trinité
Arradon
VANNES
Locmariaquer
Port-Navalo
Quiberon
St-Gildas-de-Rhuys
Sarzeau
Belle-Île
le Palais
Locmaria
Houat
Hoëdic
Questembert
Rochefort-en-Terre
Allaire
Muzillac
la Roche-Bernard
Pénestin
la Gacilly
Redon
Vilaine
Vivier-sur-Mer
Pte du Grouin
Cancale
le Mont-St-Michel
Dol-de-Bretagne
Antrain
Combourg
Canal d'Ille et Rance
Bécherel
Couesnon
Fougères
St-Aubin-d'Aubigné
St-Aubin-du-Cormier
Montauban-de-Bretagne
Montfort
RENNES
Vitré
Plélan-le-Grand
Châteaugiron
Guichen
Maure
la Guerche
Pipriac
Messac
Grand-Fougeray
Châteaubriant
St-Julien-de-Vouvantes
la Chapelle-Gl
Guémené-Penfao
Plessé
Nozay
Riaillé
St-Gildas-des-Bois
Blain
Joué
Herbignac
Pontchâteau
Nort
Ligné
Boulay
Guérande
le Croisic
la Baule
St-Nazaire
Pornichet
Savenay
Ancenis
St-Etienne-de-Montluc
la Chapelle
Carquefou
Paimbœuf
St-Père-en-Retz
St-Herblain
NANTES
St-Julien-de-Coucelles
Rezé
Pte de St-Gildas
Pornic
Arthon
Lac de Grand Lieu
Vallet
Clisson
Aigrefeuille
Bourgneuf
St-Philibert-de-Grand-Lieu
29
22
56
35
44
N
ATELIER DE CARTOGRAPHIE DES ÉDITIONS GISSEROT
0
30 km

Index

Le chiffre 1 correspond à la couverture, et 64 au dos de la couverture